THE IMMATERIAL BOOK
of
ST. CYPRIAN

FOLK CONCEPTS & VIEWS ON *The Book* AS A CULTURAL
ITEM THROUGH THE READING OF FOLK NARRATIVES

Compiled and translated by

José Leitão

REVELORE PRESS
SEATTLE
2017

The Immaterial Book of St. Cyprian:
Folk Concepts and Views on The Book as a Cultural Item
through the Reading of Folk Narratives

© José Leitão 2017.

Second volume of the Folk Necromancy in Transmission series
conceived and curated by Dr Alexander Cummins and Jesse Hathaway Diaz.

Book and cover design by Joseph Uccello.

The map of Portugal that forms the basis for the cover design and that appears in full
on page 36 was originally found on page 18 of Charles Smith, *Smith's New General
Atlas Containing Distinct Maps of all the Principal Empires, Kingdoms, & States
throughout the world carefully delineated from the best authorities extant* (London,
1808). Image © 2000 Cartography Associates in the David Rumsey Map Collection:
www.davidrumsey.com

ISBN 978-1-947544-05-5
Printed in the United States of America.

First published by Rubedo Press in May 2017.

REVELORE PRESS

220 2nd Ave S #91
Seattle, WA 98104
United States

www.revelore.press

CONTENTS

Acknowledgements

I am not a man to give public thanks or dedicate anything to anyone. That is an unhygienic habit. However, falling into a cliché, I have to admit that there really are people without whom this book would not exist. So, from that perspective, it somehow seems appropriate to write something here. The first of these would be Jenn Zahrt, closely followed by the Revelore Press team; this whole project was originally just a half-baked idea I had one day while on the prowl for Dutch spiced cookies. Jenn immediately saw the potential in it, and it is her responsibility that I actually sat down to write it. Fabio Silva was also tremendous for giving this book a second read and offering an archeologist's opinion. And finally Saint Bavo; independently of space, *ik ben een Haarlemmer* and so is this book.

INTRODUCTION

¶When we talk about 'tradition', there is a concrete limit to where mulling over books and texts can take us. Tradition runs in overly human channels of experience. Emotions, baseline feelings appear to want to trigger a callback to something slightly less civilized and intellectual. Strange and diffuse ghosts of semi-forgotten and never psychoanalyzed experiences that the word 'tradition' – as referring to something (hopefully) tangible – cannot even really encompass. So maybe, it is more useful to stop talking about 'tradition' altogether, as if this word has any concrete, universal, and intrinsic meaning, and start talking about experience.

Experience is by definition personal and non-transmissible; it is not open to criticism, judgment or (more importantly) weaponization. Instead of saying 'I follow this tradition', as if this means something and makes you special, it might be better to say 'I seek this experience', the formalities of which are your own business.

What is then hoped in this current book is to discuss and present a certain variety of experience; magical some might say, but, in my perspective, simply human. *The Book of St. Cyprian* as a traditional book of magic – or simply as a

traditional object of authority – has a certain kind of experience associated with it. Several, actually: the experience of holding it, the experience of reading it, the experience of practicing it, but before all of these, the very experience of it. The highs and lows of fear and taboo, all of which frames the experience of *The Book of St. Cyprian* as a concept beyond the circumstantial words written in it.

But in fact, what is the Portuguese *Book of St. Cyprian*? This question has no simple answer and a number of people, from a variety of backgrounds, locations, and time frames could give different answers and none would be wrong. Yet, surprisingly, the simplest answer is that *The Book of St. Cyprian* is a book of magic – but this answer is only admissible because it transports the problem into that of what magic is.

Contrary to what some weaponizing traditionalists will occasionally claim, there is no answer for what magic is. Historically speaking, magic is a fluid concept; every moment, culture, environment, society and individual will have its own definition. 'Magic' can be observed to be an umbrella term used almost arbitrarily to cover a number of other concepts, practices and experiences which have close to nothing to do with each other; except of course that they are associated with the same word.[1] Yet, it is precisely because of this that the above answer is correct: *The Book of St. Cyprian* is a book of magic, of all the magic.

This book exists in a continuum tied to the name of a mysterious Sorcerer Saint: from the plays of Gil Vicente in

---

1 See Otto and Stausberg, eds., *Defining Magic: A Reader.*

the sixteenth century,[2] to the records of the Inquisition,[3] to wild and freeform books of treasures-hunting and folk magic, dictatorial censorship offices in the twentieth century, to finally the free market of ideas and concepts. All that any person in any of these periods and environments called magic is admissible in *The Book of St. Cyprian*. Thus, in any period or place, in Portugal, Iberia, or South America, *The Book* is the repository of non-assumed authority. But of course authority is not universal (contrarily to what weaponizing traditionalists might again argue), and it is tightly linked to a particular culturally located code of values. The particular case of *The Book* then becomes increasingly complex to unravel when large sections of the code it carries, across its uncountable variations, are by definition unwritten and often unspoken. As in many cultures, this code can nonetheless be sought in its sacred literature: the stories, tales, legends, myths, and the unconceptualized impact of space from which these primarily arise.[4] The thin borders between the open and assumed practiced religion and those other things priests will avoid talking about so as not to lose their flocks. The inner feelings of a less-than-Christian nature you keep silent about but that everyone knows everybody else also has.

We may all pick this book up in our current modern comforts of warm water and heated food, and at times forget just how long its history is. The travels it took for this book to be here right now, in convenient print and typeset.

---

2 Vicente, *Exortação da Guerra*, 157a.

3 Paiva, *Bruxaria e Superstição num País Sem 'Caça às Bruxas'*, 165.

4 And its atmosphere, in the Spareian sense.

The Book of St. Cyprian, in its travels, always leaves behind footprints. No environment where *The Book* has entered can hope to pass unoffended, and our current one will not be the exception. To try to understand the nature of this book – its experience, or at least part of it – some of these footprints need to be looked at. Those cast in the times when this book was not simply a commodity that could be bought and sold, when night meant a darkness that no light could break, when civilization was small and the mountain immense. The knowledge of the certainty of a Devil and an infinity of other inhumanities roaming the wilderness, the remote and ragged cliffs of endless echoes no one will ever hear, the clarity of the right and wrong of a society, the will to cross this border and its cost – this is the habitat of the experience we want to explore here.

We are left aiming at explaining concepts of unconceptualized words in order to find some hints or clues to aid us in acquiring some kind of understanding of *The Book of St. Cyprian*. In this current attempt we will focus on folk legends and accounts that explicitly feature *The Book* as a concrete element in their narrative. By looking at these code-carrying footprints, it is hoped we may catch a glimpse of what images and ideas the mention of *The Book* would evoke in someone from an environment in which it naturally exists.

DEFINITIONS & SOURCE MATERIAL

¶Given the number of interpretations, articulations, and uses given to various forms of traditional narratives in or out of academic, as well as practitioner circles (legend, tale, story, or myth and all its Eliadian significance), a definition of 'legend' as used in the current work should first and foremost be supplied. Following what appears to be the common definition being used by Lusophone folk researchers (Alexandre Parafita or Rúbia Lóssio for example), the word 'legend' here will refer to a narrative of events whose base is taken as factual. It is possible for a 'legend' to be geographically located, even if its facts and its location in time may be murky and given different forms or interpretations.[5] Within this definition, and analyzing the legends below, I will not be making allegorical or psychological readings of these narratives – an approach which I, in fact, largely reject, mostly because these narratives, when reported by their communities, do not really symbolize or represent anything beyond themselves and the description of a certain environment or experience, frequently related to toponymy. To project and enforce meaning into a narrative beyond that given to it by its natural holders (as if calling these ignorant of their own culture) is to engage in the most abhorrent form of cultural colonialism.

---

5 Marques, *Mouras, Mouros e Mourinhos Encantados em Lendas do Norte e Sul de Portugal*, 1:9.

All of the folk legends presented below were collected from the website *Lendarium*, or 'The Archive of Portuguese Legends,' a project of the Centro de Estudos Ataíde Oliveira belonging to the University of the Algarve.[6] From this, 31 'items' containing references to *The Book of St. Cyprian* were collected and were subsequently translated and organized into a specific order, including some that are alternative versions of each other. The titles given are those provided in the *Lendarium* website.

PRESENTATION & THEMES

¶On these legends themselves, the first three items presented are meant to contribute to the specific understanding of what it means to possess and use of *The Book of St. Cyprian*, with possible overlaps into issues of social roles or stigma. The recurrent conception emerging from the reading of this collection of legends is that of how possession of *The Book* marks an individual as breaking the norm. Legend [1] is a perfect example of this. Its protagonist, described as a 'very shy boy', is presented as one who breaks away from the general expected behavior of a man. He fails to conform to expectations of virility and, more importantly, *machismo*. Yet, as part of the 'package' of his underdeveloped masculinity, comes what appears to be a natural possession and understanding of *The Book*. The protagonist, although driven by desperation (another recurrent topic, such as in legend [9]),

6 http://www.lendarium.org/; http://www.ceao.info/

does not read *The Book* in the hopes of discovering its mystery, he reads it in search of a solution, meaning that it had no mystery to him, the only question being its application.

Likewise, legend [2], while not really a legend so much as a folk account of what a *bruxa* (witch) is supposed to be (not extensive nor complete by any means), defines these mostly by their possession of *The Book*: a woman does not acquire *The Book* because she is a *bruxa*, she is a *bruxa* because she has *The Book*. *The Book* is the mark of a *bruxa*'s non-normality, it is not an object intended for those who fit into a more normalized and accepted social role. Not only this, but this particular item also offers a number of elements that I have not yet found in any other folk account regarding *bruxas*. Besides their nature as magical women, what is also suggested here is a very deep concrete difference between a *bruxa* and any other typical human, even on a physical level. This connects with legend [3], offering yet another parallel between the Portuguese witch and the Portuguese werewolf.

Legend [3], hailing from the Portuguese South and featuring a folk account of a *lobisomem* (werewolf), requires some consideration. First off, its geographical location should be taken into account since the overwhelming majority of items collected are from the Portuguese North. This by itself offers something on the geographical distribution of *The Book* as a folk concept. Like the previous two, the individual in question, believed to be a *lobisomem*, is simply reported as having *The Book*, as if this is an inherent aspect of this state. What is interesting regarding his nature as a *lobisomem*, meaning, a man who can transform into something else (the Portuguese accounts, including those of the Algarve, most

often mention the werewolf's transformation as being into a donkey), is that, in this particular account, this character-istic has absolutely no impact on what is being narrated.[7] Effectively the image of the *lobisomem* as transmitted here is largely that of a male *bruxa*, both of which are the result of parallel 'remarkable birth' circumstances in Portuguese accounts. Typically a *lobisomem* is the seventh son of a couple who only had male children, given that his name is not Bento or Custodio (other variations exist), or that one of his brothers is not his godfather.[8] On the opposite side of the spectrum, the seventh daughter of a couple who only had female children and is not named Benta or Custodia and whose godmother is not one of her sisters will be a *bruxa*.

This piece of lore is far from being monolithic, as similar seventh (or ninth) son circumstances may also be conducive to a child being a *bento* (a blessed, which is the literal trans-lation of one of the names meant to ward off werewolfism), as mentioned by José Pedro Paiva and meaning a healer whose power originates from a divine source.[9] Likewise, seventh daughter can also be placed as a specific kind of *bruxa*, a *Peeira* or *Lobeira*, a wolf shepherdess.[10] This particu-lar circumstance at times is also described as being limited to seven years, during which the Peeira will live with a pack of wolves and feed on their milk, as also the *fado* (fate, karma, or destiny) of a *lobisomem* can be time constrained.[11]

7 Nova, *As Lendas do Sobrenatural da Região do Algarve*, 1:68.
8 Vasconcelos, *Tradições Populares de Portugal*, 262.
9 Paiva, *Bruxaria e Superstição num País Sem 'Caça às Bruxas'*, 165.
10 Vasconcelos, *Tradições Populares de Portugal*, 261.
11 Vasconcelos, *Etnografia Portuguesa*, 7:386.

To further intertwine the notion of *lobisomem* and *bruxa*, the most typical method of breaking this *fado* is to make the *lobisomem* bleed during his transformed state, which will cause him to revert to his human nature permanently.[12] This exact same circumstance is then also reported in legend [2], as also in a few rare Portuguese Inquisition records where *bruxas* are mentioned as shape shifters, as given by Paiva.[13] However, contrasting with the *bruxa*, who can be indirectly or magically counter-acted, the *lobisomem*, by his male condition (as given by legend [3]) is subjected to the violence of men as a counter-measure.

The topic of the *lobisomem* is vast, and the point here is not to exhaust it in any way. Not wanting to stray excessively from the main topic of this work, a large amount of information on *lobisomens* was of course collected by José Leite de Vasconcelos and published in his *Etnografia Portuguesa*, although he directs his reader mostly to the work of Consiglieri Pedroso.[14] This last gentleman was the only individual out of his generation to have tried to approach the topic of the *lobisomem* in a more coherent and systematic way for his *Contribuições para uma Mitologia Popular Portuguesa*.[15] Unfortunately, as was the trend of his generation, he tends to constantly relate any piece of collected information with some other central European account or, even worse, a clas-

12 Ibid.
13 Paiva, *Bruxaria e Superstição num País Sem 'Caça às Bruxas'*, 146.
14 See Vasconcelos, *Etnografia Portuguesa*, 7:385–96; also, for an insight on Vasconcelos' character as a researcher and an overview on his approaches towards *The Book of St. Cyprian* see Leitão, 'Searching for Cyprian in Portuguese Ethnography', 117–62.
15 See Pedroso, *Contribuições para uma Mitologia Popular Portuguesa*, 183–96.

sical Greek or Roman one, muddying up his own fieldwork with a large amount of references and quotes which add nothing to the actual topic being discussed. Beyond these, I can recommend some of the work of Francisco Vaz da Silva to the interested reader. His papers on Portuguese seven son traditions are quite remarkable (with the advantage of having been written in English).[16]

Overall, the topic of *The Book* as an object identifying a kind of social exceptionality or non-normality is hinted at numerous other times in the remaining legends ([6], [7], [14], [16]). In these, either a priest, a witch, or an otherwise 'specialist' whose behavior and drive is distinct from the 'protagonists', needs to be sought in order to work with *The Book*.

Returning to the remaining legends, legend [4] is taken from the remarkable *Portugal Antigo e Moderno* by Pinho Leal (as also legend [13]), a monumental work of nineteenth-century chorography. This means that it is not presented according to any form of current academic 'non-judgmental methodology', but it is intended to be a good introduction to the topic which makes up the majority of legends presented: that of magical treasure-hunting and its connection to *Mouras Encantadas*.

16 See Vaz da Silva, 'Extraordinary Children, Werewolves, and Witches in Portuguese Folk Tradition', 255–68; Vaz da Silva, 'Iberian Seventh-Born Children, Werewolves, and the Dragon Slayer', 335–53.

MOURAS & TREASURE

¶*Mouras* and their treasures are complex things to describe.
I have attempted this in the past, with some success, yet
it also seems appropriate to offer some elements here in
order to shed more light on the narratives gathered in this
collection.[17] *Mouras*, to first offer a reduced and far-from-
accurate conception, can be regarded as the Portuguese
equivalent of Fairies and other such figures. However, these
and their folk stories can best be understood to fit into a
certain spectrum, which is not homogeneous everywhere in
Iberia.

On one end of this spectrum are what are usually called
the 'historical *mouras*', although I personally prefer to refer
to these as semi-historical (exemplified in legends [4], [5]
and [12]). This aspect describes them as the old rulers of the
Iberian Peninsula before the *Reconquista* and the establish-
ment of the several Christian kingdoms which would eventually result in the current Portugal and the several Spanish
nations. These were the daughters of powerful Moorish
rulers, cruel and versed in dark magic who – either due to
the forbidden love of their daughters for a Christian knight,
or out of fear of losing their possessions to the conquering
Christians – enchanted these damsels into a state of neither
living nor dying. They were then placed as eternal treasure
guardians waiting to be freed by the brave man willing to

17 Leitão, *The Book of St. Cyprian*, 264–73.

perform the complex test of courage known as the disenchantment.

On the other end of the spectrum is the 'mythical *moura*'.
Narratives and accounts featuring these typically offer no
explanation for their existence or placement as treasure
keepers (such as legends [13], [14], [15], [16], [17], [21], [22] and
[24]). These *Mouras*, most frequent in the Portuguese North,
are understood simply as being ancient, something that
survived from another age and is kept in a neither-neither
state by an evil enchantment or mysterious *fado*. Thus these
translate an idea of a certain alien strangeness. From a folk
perspective, all which somehow falls outside of a commu-
nity's collective memory or identity is ascribed to these
mythical *Mouras* and *Mouros*. All pre-Christian constructions, from prehistoric standing stones and hill forts to
Roman ruins, are the constructions of the ancient *Mouros*:
the all-encompassing 'others' used in the construction of 'us'
by opposition. They can then be described as either giants
or dwarfs (*Maruxinhos*), long gone or merely hiding in old,
ruined, and wild places such as caves or natural or ancient
water basins (legends [8], [11] and [26]). They and their immense riches are then often associated with and sought in
ancient megalithic structures and local landmarks (legend
[17]), strange and unusual natural formations such as boulders (legends [1], [10], [17], [22], [25] and [27]) and barrows
(legends [1], [7], [11] and [13]). Notable activities of *Mouras*
associated with these places would be those of weaving (legends [16] and [21]) and drying out clothes and objects under
the night sky (legend [12]). All along this spectrum, from
'historical' to 'mythical', a theme which recurs with *Mouras*

is their position as anti-Christians, be it through their pagan
or Moorish roots, being thus frequently associated directly
with the Devil (legends [7], [9], [24], [30] and [31]), who is also
the natural guardian of buried treasure. Related to this is
the depiction of *Mouras* as seductive and dangerous, pre-
senting themselves in activities and forms which transgress
the social norms of a Christian woman. Associated with
this erotic element, one other common theme in the North
of Iberia and eventually Brazil (although not so much the
Iberian South) is the description of the enchanted *Moura* as
a serpent.[18] Building upon their erotic and sexual character,
these serpent *Mouras* typically present themselves with the
intention of being kissed or have some kind of oral con-
tact with their potential male disenchanter, occasionally
described as an opportunity to suck his baptismal oils as a
means of regaining human form.[19]

Their pre-Christian presentation is also highlighted by
another recurrent point of disenchantment: namely St.
John's Eve (legends [15], [21] and [28]). In the Portuguese
North (as in most other places), this is a festival of rites of
great sexual connotation, with many forms of love magic
and divination *par excellence* being performed at this time.[20]
In terms of magical practices, this specific night is of course
considered particularly significant for achieving a number
of culturally-located motives: this is, for instance, the night

18 Marques, *Mouras, Mouros e Mourinhos Encantados em Lendas do Norte e Sul de
      Portugal*, 1:48.
19 Contreiras, *As Lendas de Mouras Encantadas*, 93, 98.
20 Leitão, *The Book of St. Cyprian*, 361.

when the Devil comes to dance around ferns.[21] What is suggested by the recurrence of the *Moura* and disenchantment motifs around St. John's Eve is that this is a liminal moment (such as midnight, mentioned in legends [20] and [27]), what Amália Marques refers to as the *hora do entreaberto* (hour of the half-open).[22] The nature of the enchantment of a *Moura* places her in a kind of limbo state between this world and some other place, and the proximity of the civilized Christian world of 'Us' to the rest of what-is-out-there – due to the liberties given to individuals in this particular night – then marks this point as the most propitious time for this kind of 'world-hopping' ritual. This 'world-hopping' does in fact function in both directions, as this is not only the appropriate time for disenchantment by humans, but also the appropriate time for *Mouras* and other *encantados* to enter the world in their true forms and seek brave would-be disenchanters.[23]

One further articulation which needs to be addressed is the male *Mouro* (present in legends [6], [9], [10] and [11]). Ranging from the semi-historical to the purely mythical, these figures are presented in folk accounts as dangerous and evil warriors, being the target of deep-seated hatred and scorn, in contrast with the always-tragic *Moura*. We find further joints and kinks along the spectrum of 'historical' to 'mythical' in the linguistic parallels between Moura/

21 Vasconcelos, *Tradições Populares de Portugal*, 109-10.
22 Marques, *Mouras, Mouros e Mourinhos Encantados em Lendas do Norte e Sul de Portugal*, 1:8.
23 Consiglieri Pedroso, *Contribuições para uma Mitologia Popular Portuguesa e Outros Escritos Etnográficos*, 219.

Moira and their activity as weavers and the Greek Moirai; or
alternatively, as proposed by Fernanda Frazão and Gabriela
Morais, the proximity of this word with the Celtic *mrvos,
meaning 'dead'.[24] The implications for the practitioner here
are of course extremely rich and exciting, as this line can
lead us into interesting explorations of remote ancestral
work which can feed back into the practice of Cyprianic
magic and treasure-hunting.

While not wanting to over-extend this presentation,
for a look into some of the possible origins of the *Moura*
as a mythical figure, I would advise the work of Roslyn M.
Frank, especially if you are a fan of the Paleolithic Continuity Refugia Paradigm.[25] Alternatively, in line with the regular
Paleolithic Continuity Paradigm, the works of the already-
mentioned Frazão and Morais are quite relevant.[26]

Beyond the *Moura/o*, the idea of the treasure itself should
be analyzed equally as a standalone concept in this environment. Legends [25], [26], and [29] present the idea of treasures being enchanted by themselves and not associated
with an *encantado* entity. The notion of *encanto* (enchantment) is multifaceted, and this particular state of being
can be seen to be imposed not only on individuals but also

---

24 Frazão and Morais, *Portugal, Mundo dos Mortos e das Mouras Encantadas*, 1:18.
25 Frank, 'Evidence in Favor of the Palaeolithic Continuity Refugium Theory (PCRT):
    Hamalau and its linguistic and cultural relatives,' Part 1, Insula 4 (2008): 91-131;
    Frank, 'Evidence in Favor of the Palaeolithic Continuity Refugium Theory (PCRT):
    Hamalau and its linguistic and cultural relatives,' Part 2, Insula 5 (2009) 89-133;
    Frank, 'Recovering European Ritual Bear Hunts: A Comparative Study of Basque
    and Sardinian Ursine Carnival Performances', Insula 3 (2008): 41-97.
26 See Frazão and Morais, *Portugal, Mundo dos Mortos e das Mouras Encantadas*;
    http://www.continuitas.org/.

objects, locations, and animals.

As defined by Parafita, to be *encantado* means to be forced into an inferior state.[27] In the case of an individual, this state translates itself as a change into an animal form, the placing of the individual under profoundly restricting taboos and modes of action or ultimate subjection to another, such as the Devil, an evil sorcerer, or the potential disenchanter. For objects and treasure, this might even take a more literal meaning, as an enchanted treasure is hidden under the earth or inside a great boulder, or under the guardianship of the Devil, demons, a long forgotten sorcery, or spirits of the dead. Digging for such a treasure and placing it within visual reach does not guarantee its physical proximity, as the *encanto* still holds and maintains it beyond the reach of individuals. Again as Parafita puts it, the treasure-as-*encanto* is transfigured as that of an illusion or mirage needing a disenchantment to be made concrete.[28]

Within this realm, otherwise inanimate objects subjected to an *encanto* can acquire zoomorphic characteristics, like humans. Typical among these are a golden calf (legends [6], [8], [29], [30] and [31]) and the chicken with the golden chicks (legend [19]), both of which are widespread in the Iberian territory and beyond to the Americas.[29] Academic consideration of the golden calf (or other types of horned cattle associated with treasure, such as the goat)[30] typi-

27 Parafita Correia, *Mouros Míticos em Trás-os-Montes*, 1:210.
28 Ibid.
29 Pedrosa, `El Cuento de El Tesoro Soñado (AT1645) y el Complejo Leyendístico de El Becerro de Oro', 127–57; Pedrosa, Palácios, and Marcos, *Héroes, Santos, Moros y Brujas*, 106.
30 See treasures 100, 106, 120, and 126 in Leitão, *The Book of St. Cyprian*, 44–45.

cally relate it to the biblical narratives of Exodus but do
not actually extrapolate any useful information from this.
Personally, I do not disagree with this observation, but in
order to understand the golden calf when placed within the
encantado world, a further step needs to be taken. Taking
the lead from the *Mouras* as an ancient entity of pre- or
anti-Christian character, the golden calf – through active en-
forcement of the Biblical narrative – can be equally seen as
a pre- or anti-Christian treasure; an unholy (but monetarily
desirable) idol left behind from an ancient time (similar to
those in legend [4]).[31]

The Chicken with Golden Chick however is a completely
unresolved mystery. While being widespread and actually having several roles and interpretations in the Iberian enchanted treasure mythology (such as a simply the
indicator of the location of a hidden treasure),[32] the possible
origin or significance of this strange treasure seems to have
eluded most scholars, with the working theory being that,
as Parafita mentions, this might be a remnant of stellar
worship.[33]

A wider analysis of the various types of other forms
assumed by *Moura* treasure in these legends may also lead
us to some familiar places. It can be observed that the more
'unremarkable' forms of treasures presented are those of
golden everyday tools such as harrows, carts, yokes (legends
[23] and [28]) and, of course, the looms with their Moirai
connections. There is an obvious labor thematic to these,

31 See treasure 16 in Leitão, *The Book of St. Cyprian*, 39.
32 López, *Tesoros, Ayalgas y Chalgueiros*, 26.
33 Parafita Correia, *Mouros Míticos em Trás-os-Montes*, 1:207.

as Parafita mentions the existence of pick-axes, knives, rifles, or scissors in other folk accounts, however the exact interpretation of this remains quite ambiguous.[34] One hypothesis is that these may be related to the nature of the enchantment and its effect over these treasures and their keepers, as all such tools, like the loom, are in fact worked by the *Moura/o* as a form of never-ending obsessive slavery. The disenchantment of these treasures would then signify the breaking of the enslaved state of the *encantado*.

Alternatively, these may be interpreted as symbolic of a Christian morality lesson, in that gold or wealth can only be found through hard work, making such tools 'golden' only by their proper non-avaricious use. I would, however, propose the exact opposite. Looking at such treasure from an anti-Christian perspective, these tools are those regularly associated with hard manual labor through which individuals can only acquire a meager living; yet here, as golden treasures, they reveal themselves as the very means for the ultimate emancipation from hard, 'virtuous' labor.

Beyond disenchantment, treasure-hunting (magical or not) should be understood as a deep-rooted practice among Iberians. Similarly to the use of *The Book*, this activity can also be seen to be mainly performed by non-native 'specialists' throughout Spain, such as Gitanos, Jews, Berbers and black men, probably until the nineteenth century.[35] Taking the Asturian example, and logically following Jesús Suárez López' insanely remarkable *Tesoros, Ayalgas y Chalgueiros*,

34 Ibid., 1:206.
35 López, *Tesoros, Ayalgas y Chalgueiros*, 30–31.

the hunting for treasure, enchanted or otherwise, has its roots in the literary tradition of the *gazetas*, *gacetas*, or *gacepas* – small manuscript books offering lists of treasures within a region and, occasionally, their method of disenchantment.[36] This type of literature is quite widespread in Europe and Iberia in particular since at least the Middle Ages, with numerous different designations being given to it, such as the Portuguese *tombos* or *roteiros*.[37] The origins of such books are at times also a vast and complex issue; such literature can be seen to be common in most of the known world. But, even if mere supposition, Peter Missler very entertainingly attempts to relate this Iberian literary current with actual Moorish treasure literature in circulation in North Africa in the ninth century.[38]

Finally, the relationship between the activity of treasure-hunting and magical disenchantment is not necessarily linear, and *gazetas* and disenchantment literature can be seen to exist as parallels to each other. As pointed out by Missler once again, these two types of books can be seen to establish, partly, a kind of literary interdependence in certain circumstances and environments, as at times one will depend on the other for either motivation or form.[39] The instance when these can perhaps be considered as strictly stand-alone items would be those of *roteiros* that include their own disenchantment methods, or disenchant-

36 Ibid., 46.
37 Pedrosa, 'El Cuento de El Tesoro Soñado (AT1645) y el Complejo Leyendístico de El Becerro de Oro', 127-57.
38 Missler, 'Las Hondas Raíces del Ciprianillo. Tercera parte', 17.
39 Ibid.

ment books existing in circumstances where the location of treasure was not dependent on literary sources (such as in legends [11] and [26]).

The treasure disenchantment sections presented in most editions of the Portuguese *Book of St. Cyprian* can then be seen as a result of these two interdependent lines of literature. The versions of *The Book* carrying the most notorious treasure-hunting sections were largely produced during the nineteenth century, precisely during the boom in *gazeta* production and enthusiasm (although these were already very well known in the eighteenth century, as mentioned by Benito Feijoo).[40] On this topic, I can do no better than suggest the already mentioned *Tesoros, Ayalgas y Chalgueiros*, where one can in fact find three full *gazeta* transcriptions, and Missler's paper on the analyses of the *Millonario de San Ciprian*.[41]

THE BOOK AS TREASURE DISENCHANTMENT

¶*The Book of St. Cyprian* can therefore be situated in this complex mythical landscape as one of the surefire methods to disenchant a treasure belonging to a *Moura/o*, and it is in this aspect that it is largely presented here. However, as pointed out by Amália Marques, the use of *The Book of*

---

40 Feyjoó y Montenegro, `De la vana y perniciosa aplicación a buscar tesoros escondidos', 10–21; López, *Tesoros, Ayalgas y Chalgueiros*, 45; See Leitão, *The Book of St. Cyprian*, 33–47, 172–82.

41 López, *Tesoros, Ayalgas y Chalgueiros*, 389–431; Missler, `Tradición y parodia en el Millonario de San Ciprián, primer recetario impreso para buscar tesoros en Galicia', 8.

St. Cyprian is just one of a number of means by which to
achieve this desired result of treasure disenchantment.[42]
Numerous other narratives simply mention tests of courage
frequently involving kissing the serpent *Moura*, feeding her
baby with Christian milk, or performing a secretive task.
Nonetheless, the use of *The Book* should also be seen in the
light of a test of courage, which is precisely related to its sta-
tus as a taboo object for any 'regular', non-magical person.
To use *The Book* as a non-specialist is always an act of courage, given the dangerous and possibly lethal side effects that
might spring from its use.

The identification of *The Book* as one method among
many to disenchant a treasure places it clearly within a wider cultural whole, and consequently cannot be understood
as a stand-alone item. Likewise its treasure-hunting sections
cannot be considered as isolated and purely literary rituals.[43] The ultimate proof of this lies in the several presenta-
tions, in the legends below, of incompatible variations on
the use of *The Book* for treasure disenchantment (legends [5],
[6], [12] and [15]). Several conclusions can be taken from this,
namely that, the treasure disenchantment ritual present in
most of the Portuguese editions is not monolithic (according to the folk understanding of it), and several disenchantment procedures using *The Book*, or simply various *Books*,
are expected to exist depending on local circumstances.
This last hypothesis is actually more than just a supposition.
Evidence has been found of a supposedly extinct variety

42 Marques, *Mouras, Mouros e Mourinhos Encantados em Lendas do Norte e Sul de
Portugal*, 1:24.
43 See Leitão, *The Book of St. Cyprian*, 33-37.

of manuscript *Books of St. Cyprian*, consisting solely of one single and extremely lengthy treasure disenchantment ritual specifically intended for priestly use (such as specifically mentioned in legend [7]).[44] As is always the case with *The Book*, there is more here than meets the eye, and the borders between legend and reality are continuously blurred in all dealings with the Sorcerer Saint. Ultimately, what this transmits is the idea of *The Book*, simply, as a mysterious thing. Its written content is indifferent, and its significance as an object of power in the hands of a specialist is almost total, even if never completely under control.

REGAINING LOST EXPERIENCES &
   CONTEXTS OF *THE BOOK*

¶From all of these various disparate ideas and concepts arises the very concrete notion of the extremely circumstantial nature and locality of *The Book*. This may be, at times, a complicated idea to fully grasp in the contemporary 'west' for a number of reasons. Globalization and demagogical discourses on the nature of democracy have covertly led many of us to think that all have the right to and capacity of understanding any piece of information and cultural item made apparently available for commercial acquisition, as the lines that once divided us as completely alien to each other have been blurred. This is not necessarily a negative

---

44 This mysterious manuscript is currently under study and should be published in my upcoming work.

thing, but we should all still remember that, in truth, we cannot really know the human experience of another without actually experiencing it, and *The Book*, like many other books, is inseparable from its human experience.

Hence, owning *The Book of St. Cyprian* or reading it as an outsider to its culture will always have its limits. The same is also true of many other folk magic books, attributed to Cyprian or not, or even purely literary and high society grimoires. Its association with *bruxas* and *lobisomens*, priests and 'specialists', is really not just a literary convention. This is a book that stands outside of social 'normality', to touch it or even merely speak of it (nevermind actually use it) is a sin, and this 'sin' extends well beyond any Christian definition. This is social and cultural sin; it is the undermining of all written, spoken, and unspoken rules and conventions of what defines a society and the rule and place of the individual within it. By reading it, studying it, or becoming a 'specialist' in it, all those around you become unable to accurately locate you in the social fabric and read your motivations and ambitions, and logically, you become the target of fear and suspicion: a witch, in its sociological sense.

One can be as romantic as one may wish with all such ideas; a rebellious and anti-social behavior certainly has its modern and sexy allure. However, most rebellious and anti-social behavior, right now and in most times, always had a concrete and understood place in society: when you break the law you do not break society, you simply assume another role within it. The level of social dissonance *The Book* implies and transmits to all those who approach it is quite a few tiers beyond this: it is unredeemable dissent from all

roles society may want to project on you, and this is always a terrifying thing, even if you like to tell yourself it is not. It should then be no surprise how a book of this nature can actually become quite political, and why it was treated as an actual danger during the clerical dictatorship of the *Estado Novo* (1933–1974).

These echoes still reverberate. They may have turned their backs on the remote and ragged cliffs but they never *left* the remote and ragged cliffs, you just do not see the cliffs anymore. And you do not see the Devil either.

The narratives I have compiled and translated below, even if largely restricted to one of its many aspects, will hopefully help to place *The Book* as the object that it was experienced as in its environment and context: the kind of images, emotions, and figures which would rush through your mind and emotional centers when you, as a native, would hear the words 'The Book of St. Cyprian'.

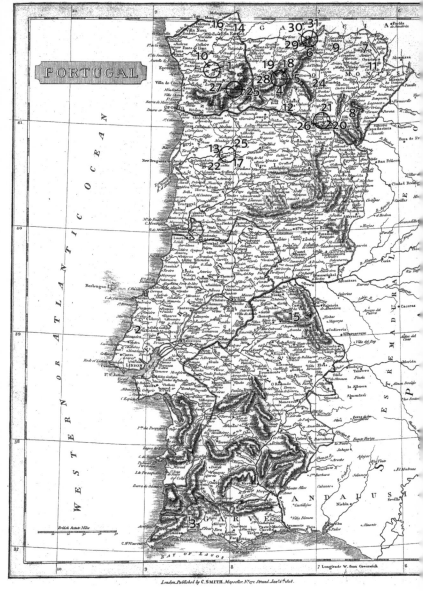

Map of the geographical locations of all folk legends presented in the following pages.

LEGENDS

[1]
A *Cova dos Mouros* †

NA ALDEIA DE MARRANCOS HAVIA um moço muito tímido que não conseguia dizer nada do que pensava. Até que se apaixonou perdidamente por uma rapariga da sua terra.

Passava junto dela e não conseguia olhar para a sua beleza. Mais tarde, conheceu-a, mas mesmo assim não conseguia sequer dizer que a achava bonita.

A vida passava para este jovem, mas a sua timidez não.

Certo dia passou por acaso na Cova dos Mouros e sentou-se a ler o Livro de São Cipriano para ver se lá encontrava alguma solução para o seu problema. Acontece que, quando acabou de o ler, lhe apareceu uma cobra. Muito assustado, picou a cobra e, para sua grande admiração, apareceu-lhe mesmo à frente uma moura encantada. Farto da sua vida, exclamou:

'Que raio havia de me acontecer! E logo eu que não faço mal a ninguém e que só pedia uma coisa na vida: casar com a minha amada'.

Para sua maior admiração, a moura olhou-o nos olhos e disse-lhe que o seu desejo seria realizado.

O moço fugiu assustado, mas o certo é que passados uns meses casou-se com a rapariga que tanto queria e sonhava.

† Origin: Braga; Source: v.a., *Literatura Portuguesa de Tradição Oral*, ME20.

[1]

The Cova of the Mouros (Mouros' Burrow)

IN THE VILLAGE OF MARRANCOS there was a very shy boy who could not express anything which was on his mind. This until he fell madly in love with a girl from his village.

He would walk past her and not even be able to look at her beauty. Later he met her, but even still, he could not even say that he found her beautiful.

Life was moving on for this boy, but his shyness wasn't.

On a certain day he passed by the Cova dos Mouros and sat there reading the *Book of St. Cyprian* to see if he could find in it some solution for his problem. It happened that, when he finished reading, a snake appeared to him. Very frightened, he stung it and, to his great admiration, an enchanted *moura* appeared right in front of him. Fed up with life he said:

'What else will happen to me! And to me of all people, I don't hurt a soul and only want one thing in life: to marry my beloved'.

For his even greater admiration, the *moura* looked him in the eyes and told him that his wish would be fulfilled.

The boy ran away frightened, but the truth is that, after a few months, he married the girl whom he so dreamed of.

Actualmente, as pessoas que têm problemas na vida, que passam por dificuldades ou mesmo que têm desejos por concretizar, vão à Cova dos Mouros, nem que seja só para ganhar a coragem de ler o Livro de São Cipriano e pensar que os seus desejos podem ser concretizados.

These days, people who have problems in life, who are going through difficulties or have a wish to fulfill, go to the Cova dos Mouros, even if only to gain courage to read the *Book of St. Cyprian* and imagine that their wishes may be fulfilled.

[2]

Bruxas †

DIZ-SE QUE AS BRUXAS ERAM mulheres que tinham O Livro de S. 'Cepriano',‡ e que de noite iam às encruzilhadas ler o tal livro e falavam com o Diabo que lhes aparecia à frente. Este ensinava-lhes 'orações' para que elas voassem, mas antes tinham que lhe beijar o 'rabo'. Só depois é que eram bruxas de verdade.

As bruxas tinham no rabo uma pequena luz que piscava e só apareciam à noite. Quem as encontrasse no caminho tinha que dizer: 'cruzes e figas' e tinha que 'fazer figas', senão as bruxas faziam com que a pessoa se perdesse.

Se por ventura um homem encontrasse uma bruxa, nunca deveria picar-lhe a tal luzinha, porque senão a bruxa transformava-se em mulher e fazia-o carregá-la às costas até a casa. Mas não podia acordar o marido dela, porque se tal acontecesse as sua companheiras matavam-no.

As bruxas, antes de saírem de casa benziam os seus maridos enquanto estes dormiam, dizendo:

'Eu te benzo com o meu "olho nu"?

Que eu vá e venha e não acordes tu'.

---

† Origin: Torres Vedras, Lisbon; Source: Morgado, *Viagens ao Imaginário*, 69.
‡ In an oral context the Portuguese 'Cipriano'/'Cypriano' may appear in a variety of forms, from the current Cepriano, Supriano (legend [2]), Ciprião or further variations on these.

[2]

Witches

IT IS SAID THAT WITCHES were women who owned *The Book of St. Cyprian*, and that at night they would go to the crossroads to read this book and talk with the Devil, who appeared to them. He would teach them prayers so they could fly, but before this they had to kiss his rear. Only after this would they become real witches.

The witches had on their rear a small blinking light, and they only appeared at night. Whoever encountered them had to say: 'crosses and figs' and had to do the fig sign, otherwise the witches would make this person lose her way. [1]

If by any chance a man would run into a witch, he should never sting this small light, for the witch would transform into a woman and make him carry her on his back to her house. But she could not wake her husband up; otherwise her companions would kill him.

Witches, before they left their houses, blessed their husbands while these slept by saying:

'I bless you with my naked eye.

May I come and go and you not awake'.

---

1 See Leitão, *The Book of St. Cyprian*, 379.

As bruxas também faziam mal às criancinhas. Dizia-se que lhes sugavam o sangue, fazendo com que perdessem o apetite. Para que isso não acontecesse, as mães nunca deixavam a roupa da criança no estendal até de noite. Era assim que as bruxas lhe deitavam o 'mau olhado'.

Muitas vezes, as pessoas mandavam sal para cima dos telhados, para que as bruxas só pudessem fazer mal a alguém depois de apanharem as pedras todas.

Witches also harmed little children. It was said that they sucked their blood, making them lose their appetite. So as this wouldn't happen, mothers never left a child's clothes drying outside into the evening. This is how the witches casted the evil eye.[2]

Often people would throw salt over their roofs, so as witches could only do them harm after they had picked all of it up.

2 This preoccupation with the exposure of children's clothes to potential evil eye is quite ancient and widespread. Particularly, this is the most common situation described for the transmission of the harmful influence of the Moon on young children, also called the *luada*, or mooning, which can be considered to be a form of lunar evil eye. On this point see Fonseca Henriquez, *Medicina Lusitana* (1710 ed), 129; Vasconcelos, *Etnografia Portuguesa*, 5:28-33 and 10:121-30.

[3]
O *João do Serro, Lobisomem* †

ALI NO RIBEIRO DO PEREIRO havia lá um homem qu'era o João Estrudes, tinha o apelido de João do Serro e tambem lhe chamavam o João Lobisome. O homem teve sempre a fama de ser lobisome, até houve quem dissesse que ele tinha embruxado o mê pai, que ele era da idade do mê pai, fizeram a tropa juntos.

Uma ocasião, lá com um sobrinho dele, que esse moço 'inda é vivo, diziam que ele andava fazendo mal ao mocito por meio do livro de S. Supriano, que havia um livro de capa verde que era o livro de S. Supriano. O pai do rapazito correu ai médicos, correu tudo, e o moço 'tava empolado, com uma grande barriga e diz que 'tava embruxado por aquele, na sei se 'tava se não. Então o pai, que era ainda mê parente, foi a caminho dele e deu-lhe tanta porrada, tanta porrada e então ou ele punha-lhe o filho bom, ou que acabava com ele.

Contanto que o mocinho foi, foi, pôs-se bom e 'inda aí está, é um moço mais novo do que eu, tem menos uns tres ou quatro anos.

† Origin: Mexilhoeira Grande, Portimão, Faro; Source: Tengarrilha, *Memória do Povo*, 36–37.

[3]
João do Serro, Werewolf

IN THE RIBEIRO DO PEREIRO there was a man called João
Estrudes, he was referred to as João do Serro and also as
João Werewolf. This man had the fame of being a werewolf,
there were even those who said he bewitched my father,
and he was the same age as him, they did their army recruit-
ment together.

On one occasion, together with his nephew, and this boy
is still alive today, people were saying that he was doing him
great harm by means of *The Book of St. Cyprian*, and this was
a book with a green cover which was the *Book of St. Cyprian*.
The father of the boy went to many doctors and to anyone
who could help, and the boy was swollen, having now a
great belly and was bewitched by that man, but I don't know
if this was such. Then his father, he was still my relative,
went to find him and beat him up so bad so as he would
either make his son well again or he would end him.

The boy went on and got better, and is still around, he is
younger than me, three or four months.

Esse tal João Lobisome levou muita porrada, de pessoas que estavem doentes e iam logo a caminho dele, e vá porrada p'ra cima. Eu vi-lhe dar tanta porrada, pois aquilo era lá ó pé de mim, tudo por modo da fama de lobisome.

Más ele, coitado, chegou lá à altura dele tambem morreu. Como era lobisome podia ainda viver mais uns anos, más ele morreu já velho, só que na lhe serviu de nada ter o livro e ser lobisome.

Más tinha mesmo a fama de ser lobisome, aquele homem. E muita gente tinha medo dele, diziam que andava à noite uivando pelos serros e que se ia encontrar com as bruxas lá nas encruzilha-das, algumas até aqui perto donde a gente agora vive, outras onde dantes eu morava, ali ao Ribeiro do Pereiro.

Uma ocasião ia eu passando lá ó pé da casa dele e vi um branquejar numa encruzilhada mais adiante. Tambem vinha eu uma vez com um irmão da minha mulher e um primo meu, nessa mesma encruzilhada que havia lá, e a gente ouviu muitos paparitos e viu aquilo a branquejar, a andar à roda. Havia de ser um baile de bruxas, mas a gente na se chegou lá ó pé. Bem, nessa altura tivemos medo, pois claro.

This João Werewolf took many beatings from people who were ill and would go immediately after him. I saw him get so many beatings, as all of this was near my place, all because he had the fame of being a werewolf.

But he, poor man, at a certain point also died. As he was a werewolf he could still live for a few more years, but he died an old man, having the book and being a werewolf was of no use to him.

But he had a great fame for being a werewolf. And many people were afraid of him, they said that he would roam the night howling through the mountains and that he would meet with witches on crossroads, some quite close by here, others from where I used to live, in Ribeiro Pereiro.

On one occasion I was passing by his house and saw some thrashing in a crossroad further ahead. Once I was also walking with a brother of my wife and a cousin of mine, on that same crossroad, and we heard great shrieking (?) and we saw that thrashing, going around in a circle. It was likely a witches' dance, but we didn't go near it. At that time we were afraid of course.

[4]
Castello ou S. Thomé do Castello †

NÃO PODIAM DEIXAR AS RUINAS d'este vetustissimo castello de ter suas lendas e contos de mouras e thesouros encantados; e o nosso bom povo, cuja imaginação é tão fertil n'estas coisas, traz ligadas a estas ruinas, historias pavorosas e horripilantes.

Ahi vão as principaes.

D. Taludo e seus antecessores possuiam riquezas hyperbolicas, que tinham escondido em uma especie de tunnell que mina o picôtto, na Fonte dos Louranços (a uns 60 metros do castello) – na Fraga dos Sabugueiros, onde se vê uma mão esquerda, por baixo da qual, diz o tombo ou roteiro, estão as armas de D. Taludo, e onde era a morada de D. Martha; na Fraga da Torre, onde ainda se vêem os alicerces de um edificio, que se diz ter sido torre, e era o carcere dos prisioneiros e delinquentes. Dista 900 a 1000 metros do castello. Por estes sitios, diz o tombo, se encontrarão as joias de um rei.

† Origin: São Tomé Do Castelo, Vila Real, Vila Real; Source: an excerpt from Pinho Leal, *Portugal Antigo e Moderno*, 2:170–71.

[4]
Castle or S. Thomé do Castello

THE RUINS OF THIS MOST ancient castle could not avoid the legends and tales of *mouras* and enchanted treasures; and our good people, whose imagination is so fertile in these things, has, connected to these ruins, fearful and horrifying stories.

Here are the principal ones.

Don Taludo and his ancestors had hyperbolic riches, which they hid in a kind of tunnel at the fountain of Louranços (some 60 meters from the castle) – in the Fraga dos Sabugueiros, where one may see a left hand, under which the 'tome' or 'guide' says there are the weapons of Don Taludo,[3] and this was the home of Lady Martha; in the Fraga da Torre, one can still see the foundations of a building, which is said to have been a tower, and this was a holding cell for prisoners and delinquents. It is 900 to 1000 meters from the castle. Around this place, the 'tome' says, one will find the jewels of a king.

---

3 This particular treasure also features in the list of treasures of *Book of St. Cyprian*, treasure 9 of the 'Places where Enchantments are to be Found' in the first part of *The Book*: «In the Castelo do Sírio, near the fountain, at the front, to the South, in the middle of the tower, two ovens built into the wall; there thou shall find the weapons of D. Teludo Seminadas, and four gold doubloons»; See Leitão, *The Book of St. Cyprian*, 38.

Tendo já fallado n'esta obra em roteiros (a que nas provincias do N. chamam tombos) é preciso dizer aos leitores que o ignorarem, que roteiro é um quaderno manuscripto que diz os sitios onde estão os thesouros encantados e a maneira de os desencantar. Já se sabe, os taes roteiros não passam de um logro.

Fiados nos taes tombos, muitos teem tentado desencantar thesouros, por meio de livros magicos (dizem que escriptos por S. Cypriano, antes da sua conversão) e com rezas dos padres, que para isso alli teem levado.

Diz-se que de uma vez acharam algumas riquezas. Que por outra vez, depois de muito trabalho nocturno, e estando mettidos todos dentro de um grande sino saimão (signo de Salomão) lhes appareceram figuras diabolicas e idolos monstruosos e medonhos, mas riquissimamente vestidos de oiro e de diamantes, que brilhavam como o sol, a cuja vista os ambiciosos desencantadores ficaram aterrados e fugiram espavoridos.

Junto á porta do castello que olhava para o N., consta que havia antigamente um buraco, por onde facilmente podia entrar um homem. Diz-se que ha annos por elle entraram varios individuos audaciosos, os quaes a poucos passos da entrada viram uma abobada de cantaria lavrada e depois umas escadas de uns 16 a 20 degraus, ao fim dos quaes se seguia uma estreita galeria até um largo onde estava um bello jardim com um elegante chafariz.

Having already mentioned in this work 'guides' (which in the provinces of the North are called 'tomes') it is necessary to explain to the unknowing readers that a 'guide' is a manuscript notebook which says where enchanted treasure is and the way of disenchanting it. One can see that such 'guides' are nothing but a hoax.

Believing in these 'tomes', many have tried to disenchant treasures, by means of magic books (which are said to have been written by St. Cyprian, before his conversion) and with prayers from priests, who are taken to these places for this practice.

It is said that one time they found some riches. One other time, after much nocturnal labor, and all of them being inside a great *sino saimão* (sign of Solomon), diabolical figures and monstrous and fearful idols appeared to them, but all of these richly dressed in gold and diamonds, which shined like the Sun, and at whose sight the ambitious disenchanters were terrified and ran.

Near the north-facing gate of the castle, it is said that there used to be a hole, through which a man could easily pass. It is said that through it many brave men entered, who, a few steps in, saw a stone dome and a further staircase of some 16 or 20 steps, after which they followed a narrow gallery until reaching a wide space with a beautiful garden and an elegant fountain.

Mais adiante estava outro largo, e n'elle um sumptuoso templo pagão, todo ornado de ouro e pedrarias, com idolos medonhos e ameaçadores que lhe faziam terriveis esgáres. Os pobres fugiram espantados, e poucos dias sobreviveram á sua temeraria empresa.

Consta que os principaes chefes d'esta expedição foram Gonçalo Esteves e Paulo Mondes, da referida aldeia de Mascusinhos, arruinada.

E lá jazem encantados os famosos e riquissimos thesouros dos antigos possuidores do castello!

Further down there was another wide space, and in it a sumptuous pagan temple, all decorated with gold and mason work, with fearful and threatening idols with terrible grimaces. The poor men ran in fear, and they only survived a few days after their terrible enterprise.

It is said that the chiefs of this expedition were Gonçalo Esteves e Paulo Mondes, of the already mentioned ruined village of Mascusinhos.

And there do lay the famous and rich treasures of the ancient owner of the castle!

[5]
Lenda da Fraga das Campainhas†

CONTA A LENDA QUE S. Cipriano deixou um livro no qual se diz que na povoação de Moreira [concelho de Vila Pouca de Aguiar] os mouros enterraram muitas riquezas, mas sempre debaixo de fragas. No lugar de Vale Bom, no Alto do Castelo, que é um conjunto de rochas todas expostas umas em cima das outras, sobressai a 'fraga das campainhas', que faz a separação dos concelhos de Vila Pouca de Aguiar e Murça. A fraga tem uma fenda arredondada ao centro, de cima para baixo, e, ao toque de qualquer objecto, parecem ouvir-se campainhas.

É aí que o livro de S. Cipriano fala que os mouros enterraram uma fortuna em ouro. Para alguém se apoderar do ouro teria de ler todas as páginas do livro sem ter medo e em redor da fraga, mas, ao lê-lo, não se podia enganar, senão nada acontecia. Por muitas vezes, houve grupos de homens que subiram até ao monte e aí começaram a ler o livro, mas poucas páginas liam, porque o medo era tanto que cada um fugia para seu lado, e só se encontravam na aldeia.

† Origin: Vila Pouca de Aguiar, Vila Real; Source: Parafita, *A Mitologia dos Mouros*, 355.

[5]
Legend of the Fraga das Campainhas (Bells' Boulder)

LEGEND SAYS THAT ST. CYPRIAN left behind a book in which it is said that, in the village of Moreira (county of Vila Pouca de Aguiar), the *mouros* buried many riches, but always under boulders. In the place of Vale Bom,[4] in the Alto do Castelo, which is a group of rocks all exposed on top of each other, the 'fraga das campainhas' (bells' boulder) stands out, which marks the border of the counties of Vila Pouca de Aguiar and Murça. The boulder has a rounded crack at its center, from top to bottom, and, when hit by any object makes a sound like a bunch of bells.

It is there that the *Book of St. Cyprian* says the *mouros* buried a fortune in gold. So as one may take this gold they would have to read all the pages of the book without fear and around the boulder, but, while reading it, one could not make a single mistake, otherwise nothing would happen. Occasionally, groups of men would go up the mount and there they would start to read the book, but they only read a few pages, for their fear was so great that each would start

4 Once again, this particular treasure also features in the list of treasures of *Book of St. Cyprian*, treasure 143 of the 'Places where Enchantments are to be Found' in the first part of *The Book*: «In the Vale Valbom, there is a large rock with a hole in it; by the side of the setting Sun, there are a hundred and forty bags of gold at the height of a man»; See Leitão, *The Book of St. Cyprian*, 46.

Um vizinho de oitenta e quatro anos disse-me que, um dia, ele e mais quatro amigos foram nessa aventura. Ele até levou uma caçadeira, mas depois de se sentarem no chão e fazerem um 'sino saimão', que era uma das recomendações do livro de S. Cipriano, um deles começou a ler, e mal tinha lido umas duas páginas ouviu-se um barulho na fenda da fraga, acompanhado de um clarão. Quando ele olhou, já se viu sozinho. Os amigos tinham fugido com medo, e ele, mesmo armado de caçadeira, também fugiu.

running in his own direction, only meeting each other back at the village.

An eighty-four year old neighbor told me that one day, he and four of his friends went on such an adventure. He even took a shotgun, but after they sat on the ground and made a *sino saimão*, which was one of the recommendations of the *Book of St. Cyprian*, one of them started reading, and as soon as he read two pages they heard a noise coming from the crack in the boulder, accompanied by a bright light. When he looked around, he was already alone. His friends had run with fear, and he, even armed with a shotgun, also ran.

[6]
O *Bezerro de Oiro* †

NA FREGUESIA DE LEBUÇÃO, CONCELHO de Valpaços, conta-se uma lenda muito antiga acerca da existência, naquela terra, de um bezerro de oiro.

Perto da povoação, há um grande penedo, em forma de boina, que, por essa razão, é chamado pedra do boné. E é dentro desse penedo, a um metro de profundidade, que está escondido um valioso tesoiro, em forma de bezerro.

O conhecimento da sua existência deve-se ao livro de S. Cipriano que fala dele na página oitenta e quatro e ensina a maneira de o conseguir tirar.

Para isso, diz o livro, é necessário juntar um grupo de homens corajosos, que não saibam o que é o medo, e, ao mesmo tempo, sérios, que sejam incapazes de se rir.

Desse grupo deve fazer parte um padre, para ler uma oração em latim, que também está escrita na página oitenta e quatro do referido livro, e deve ser lida exactamente quando for meia noite.

Se essa oração for bem rezada, sem faltar qualquer palavra nem qualquer sílaba, e o penedo for aspergido com bastante água benta, e se ninguém se rir nem sentir medo,

† Origin: Lebução, Valpaços, Vila Real; Source: Ferreira, *Lendas e Contos Infantis*, 24–26.

60

[6]
The Golden Calf

IN THE PARISH OF LEBUÇÕES, county of Valpaços, there is an ancient legend about the existence, in that land, of a golden calf.

Near this village, there is a great boulder, shaped like a bonnet, which, for that reason, is called the rock of the bonnet. Inside that boulder, one meter deep, a valuable treasure is hidden, in the shape of a calf.

The knowledge of its existence is due to the *Book of St. Cyprian*, which mentions it on page eighty-four and teaches the way to get it out.

To do this, the book says it is necessary to put together a group of brave men who do not know what fear is, and, at the same time, are serious enough and incapable of laughter.

A priest should be a part of this group, so as to read a prayer in Latin, which is also written on page eighty-four of the mentioned book, and it needs to be read exactly at midnight.

If that prayer is said without any word or syllable being missed, and the boulder is sprayed with plenty of holy water, and nobody laughs or feels fear, then the earth will violently shake, the rock will crack and the golden calf will appear.

então a terra estremecerá com violência, a pedra rachará ao meio e o bezerro de oiro aparecerá.

Mas, acrescenta ainda o livro, se alguma destas condições faltar, o tesoiro ficará irremediavelmente escondido para sempre, porque a tentativa não se pode repetir. E, pior ainda, os que fizerem parte do grupo sofrerão pesado castigo pelo seu atrevimento.

Por estas razões, se o desejo de extrair o tesoiro do penedo era muito grande, o receio de falhar e de sofrer o anunciado castigo era ainda maior.

Deste modo, rolaram os séculos, sucederam-se as gerações, sem que alguém ousasse meter ombros à arriscada aventura de enfrentar o terrível Moiro que guardava ciosamente o fabuloso tesoiro da pedra do boné.

Mas um belo dia, apareceu um filho da terra que tinha tanto de valente como de ambicioso e se mostrou disposto a correr o risco, convencido de que seria capaz de conseguir apoderar-se do tesoiro.

Juntou os vizinhos e anunciou-lhes a sua determinação, afirmando que estava decidido a tentar a empresa nem que tivesse de ir sozinho.

A sua extraordinária coragem contagiou alguns deles que se mostraram dispostos a acompanhá-lo.

Faltava, porém, o padre, elemento fundamental do grupo, e sem ele nada poderiam fazer, pois, além de não saberem ler a oração em latim, não tinham a estola e a água benta, que também faziam parte das condições impostas pelo livro.

Foram então ter com o pároco da freguesia, que também não era peco e não tinha medo do Diabo, e convenceram-no a acompanhá-los.

But, the book adds, should any of these conditions not be met, the treasure will be forever hidden, because one cannot repeat the attempt. And, worse still, those who were part of the group will suffer a heavy punishment for their daring.

For these reasons, even if the desire to extract the treasure from the boulder is great, the fear of failing and suffering the mentioned punishment is even greater.

In this way, centuries went by, generations passed, without anyone daring to take on the risky venture of facing the terrible Mouro who greedily guards the fabulous treasure of the rock of the bonnet.

But one fine day, a son of the land appeared who had as much bravery as ambition and showed himself willing to take the chance; convinced that he would be capable of taking possession of the treasure.

He gathered his neighbors and told them of his resolution, claiming that he was willing to take on this enterprise even if alone.

His extraordinary courage infected some of them, who then offered to accompany him.

They were missing, however, the priest, a fundamental element of the group, and without this they could do nothing, because, not only did they not know how to read the prayer in Latin, they did not have a stole and holy water, which is also part of the conditions placed by the book.

They then went to the village priest, who was also no coward and was not afraid of the Devil, and they convinced him to accompany them.

They armed themselves with firearms and other instruments of defense as protection from whatever might come.

Preveniram-se com armas de fogo e outros instrumentos de defesa, para o que desse viesse. E o padre encarregou-se de levar o livro de S. Cipriano, a estola e a água benta.

Partiram da aldeia, após o anoitecer, em segredo, para não serem seguidos por curiosos indesejáveis que iriam estragar tudo. E, quando chegaram junto do penedo, esperaram.

Quando a meia noite foi anunciada pelos galos da aldeia, que nisso eram infalíveis, o coração de todos deixou de bater e a respiração parou.

Então, o padre pôs a estola solenemente, abriu o livro na página oitenta e quatro e começou a dizer vagarosamente, para não se enganar, a oração em latim:

Petrus, petra, petrum,
Abre-te unum metrum.
Guarda tibi Mourum
E dá nobis tesourum.

A oração terminou e... nada: nem o mais ligeiro movimento nem o mais leve ruído. Todos começaram a ficar incrédulos.

Mas, quando o padre pegou no hissope, o mergulhou na caldeirinha e aspergiu os quatros cantos do penedo, parecia a fim do mundo.

A terra começou a tremer debaixo dos pés, como se fosse um terramoto; e o penedo, a rachar ruidosamente, como se fosse um trovão.

Então, tomados de pânico, sem esperar que o penedo se abrisse, largaram tudo e abalaram, como um raio, encosta abaixo, até chegarem à povoação.

And the priest was charged with taking the *Book of St. Cyprian*, the stole, and the holy water.

They left the village after sunset, in secret, so as not to be followed by undesirable peepers who would ruin the whole thing. And when they got to the boulder they waited.

When midnight was announced by the village roosters, which are infallible in this, everyone's heart and breath stopped.

Then, the priest solemnly put his stole on, opened the book to page eighty-four and started to slowly read, so as not to make a mistake, the Latin prayer.

Petrus, petra, petrum,
Abre-te unum metrum.
Guarda tibi Mourum
E dá nobis tesourum.

The prayer ended and... nothing: not even the slightest movement or the slightest noise. All started to become doubtful.

But, when the priest picked up the aspergillum, dipped it in the little bucket, and sprayed the four corners of the boulder, it was like the end of the world had begun.

The earth started to shake under their feet, as if it was an earthquake; the boulder started to crack as loudly as a thunder.

Then, taken by panic, without waiting for the boulder to open, everyone dropped everything and took off, as lightning, down the hill until they got to the village.

Por causa disso, por não terem a coragem de esperar até ao fim, eles ficaram tolhidos para toda a vida e o tesoiro ficou perdido para sempre no interior do penedo, porque a experiência não pode ser repetida, como diz o livro de S. Cipriano na página oitenta e quatro.

Because of this, for not having the courage to wait until the end, they became paralyzed for life and the treasure was lost forever inside the boulder, for this experiment cannot be repeated, as is mentioned in the *Book of St. Cyprian* on page eighty-four.

[7]
O *Cabeço da Velha* †

NA BASE POENTE DO CABEÇO da Velha (em Labiados, concelho de Bragança), junto à margem do rio Contense, sítio chamado Rachas, fica a Pala dos Mouros, também dita Pena Veladeira, sob a qual há uma gruta, a pala no dizer do povo, que pode acobertar um rebanho de quarenta ovelhas (...)

Pelos anos de 1860 foram desencantar a riqueza do Cabeço da Velha uns quantos sonhadores de tesouros, naturais de Baçal e Sacoias, acompanhados de um padre e de uma bruxa (...). Ainda conheci o padre, a bruxa (tia Martinha, de Sacoias) e os homens, o tio Vicente e o tio Nicolau, aquele de Sacoias e este empregado na máquina de destilação de vinhos de Baçal.

O padre era natural de Baçal, onde faleceu em 1892, e muitas vezes me contou o caso. Ele lia, lia no Livro de S. Cipriano, o autêntico, um códice antigo, manuscrito, se bem me recordo, pois os modernos, impressos, nada valem, dizia ele, e exorcizava sem cessar (é também condição indispensável), metido dentro de um pentalfa inscrito num círculo que traçou no terreno, do qual não podia sair, sob pena de ficar tudo sem efeito; a bruxa, dentro de um signo Salomão, fazia conjuros e deitava as varinhas do condão e os homens cavavam, cavavam, sem parar e calados.

† Origin: Bragança, Bragança; Source: Parafita, *A Mitologia dos Mouros*, 215-16.

[7]
The Cabeço of the Velha (Mound of the Old Woman)

AT THE WESTERN BASE OF the Cabeço da Velha (in Labiad-os, county of Bragança) near the shore of the River Con-tense, in a place called Rachas, there is the Pala dos Mouros, also called Pena Veladeira, under which there is a cave, which, in the descriptions given by the locals, can fit a flock of forty sheep (...)

Around the 1860s a few dreamers went to disenchant the riches of the Cabeço da Velha, coming from Baçal and Sacoias, accompanied by a priest and a witch (...) I still met the priest, the witch ('aunty' Martinha, from Sacoias) and the men, uncle Vicente and uncle Nicolau, the first was from Sacoias and the latter was a worker in a wine distillery in Baçal.

The priest was from Baçal, where he died in 1892, and told me of the event many times. He read the *Book of St. Cyprian*, the real one, an old manuscript tome, if I recall cor-rectly, because the modern printed ones are worthless, he said, and he exorcised without ceasing (this is also an indis-pensable condition), standing inside a pentagram inscribed in a circle he drew on the ground, from which he could not move, under the penalty of foiling the effort; the witch, inside a *sino Salomão*, was making conjurations and casting magic rods and the men were digging, digging, without stop-ping and in silence.

69

Tudo corria admiravelmente, indicando que o tesouro estava prestes a sair. Neste momento surge na escavação um sapo enorme, colossal (era o diabo, guarda do tesouro), a abrir e fechar a boca, num gesto de os papar a todos. Os homens aterram-se, o padre recua um pouco, saindo do círculo, a bruxa faz o mesmo e de repente a trincheira esboroa-se, apanhando o Nicolau pelas pernas; o tesouro, uma enorme bola de oiro, maior que a roda de um carro, reguinga pela ladeira abaixo, até se esfrangalhar no rio, sentindo-se nitidamente o tilintar do oiro nos fraguedos e lajes das margens, e um medonho tufão arrasta os sonhadores, por cima de carrascos e fraguedos, a muitos metros de distância, deixando-os assaz maltratados e sem poderem regressar a casa no mesmo dia ou só muito tarde.

A bruxa, porém, foi vista logo em Sacoias, sã e escorreita, com a cantarinha debaixo do braço a ir buscar água à fonte. E sempre assim! O tesouro lá está, dizem os da carolice; falta, porém, a coragem precisa para o desencantar.

All was going admirably, indicating that the treasure was about to appear. At this time, from the digging emerges an enormous frog, colossal (this was the Devil, guarding the treasure), opening and closing its mouth, in a movement as if wanting to gobble them up. The men were filled with dread, the priest stepped back, leaving the circle, the witch did the same and all of a sudden the ditch covered itself up, trapping Nicolau by the legs; the treasure, an enormous sphere of gold, bigger than the wheel of a cart, fell down the slope, until it crashed into the river, where one clearly heard the ringing of gold in the boulders and crags of the shores, and a fearful wind dragged all the dreamers over the crags and boulders, many meters away, leaving them very badly treated and unable to return home that same day, or, at the least, very late.

The witch, however, was seen immediately in Sacoias, fine and healthy, with her pot under her arm on the way to the fountain to fill it with water. This always happens! The treasure is still there, they say; what is missing is the courage to disenchant it.

[8]

A Moura e o Bezerro de Ouro †

HÁ NO FELGAR UM LUGAR chamado Olhadela, situado na margem direita do rio Sabor, onde existem restos de um muro que antigamente tinha três argolas de ferro para os mouros prenderem os cavalos. Também lá existe um grande buraco, a que o povo chama 'cisterna'.

Conta a lenda que nessa cisterna há uma moura encantada e um tesouro e que, para os encontrar, é preciso ir lá de noite com o livro de S. Cipriano. Já dois homens do Felgar lá foram a saber do tesouro. Chegaram, desenharam no chão um sino saimão e puseram dentro dele umas pedras para se sentarem enquanto liam o livro. E tudo estava a correr bem, até que, no meio de grandes estrondos, apareceu a moura com o bezerro de ouro.

Um dos homens, ao ouvir tamanhos estrondos, teve tanto medo, que só soube dizer:

'Valha-nos aqui Deus!'

Ditas tais palavras tudo desapareceu. E os dois homens foram atirados pelo ar, indo parar muito longe dali: um foi ter à Amarela e o outro à Fonte Salgueiro rumo à aldeia. Nunca mais se atreveram a voltar lá.

† Origin: Felgar, Torre de Moncorvo, Bragança; Source: Parafita, *A Mitologia dos Mouros*, 333.

[8]

The Moura and the Golden Calf

IN FELGAR THERE IS A place called Olhadela, located in the right shore of the River Sabor, where there are the remains of a wall which used to have three iron rings the *mouros* used to tie their horses. There is also a great hole there, which the locals call a cistern.

Legend has it that in this cistern there is an enchanted *moura* and a treasure and that, to find them, it is necessary to go there at night with the *Book of St. Cyprian*. Two men from Felgar tried to discover this treasure. They arrived, drew a *sino saimão* on the ground and placed themselves inside with some rocks so as to be sitting while they read form the book. Everything was going fine, until, in the middle of great noises, the *moura* appeared with a golden calf.

One of the men, upon hearing such loud noises, was so afraid that he could only say:

'God help us here!'

Saying these words, everything disappeared. And the two men were thrown into the air, ending up very far away from there: one went all the way to Amarela and the other to Fonte Salgueiro on the way to the village. They never again had the courage to go back there.

[9]
O *Tesouro da Cerca* †

DIZIAM OS MAIS ANTIGOS DE Gestosa de Lomba que, num lugar chamado Cerca, onde viveram os mouros, havia um tesouro enterrado e que no livro de S. Cipriano se dizia como encontrá-lo. Ora, como só o padre sabia ler o livro, uns poucos de homens da povoação pediram-lhe que fosse lá com eles a ver se davam com o tesouro.

O padre aceitou. O pior é que um deles teria de entregar, em troca, a alma ao diabo. E voluntários não os havia. Resolveram então fazer a proposta a um galego que andava a trabalhar por estes lados e que aceitou logo, pois era muito pobre e tinha a família na sua terra a passar necessidade.

E lá foram numa certa noite. Os homens escavavam, escavavam, e o padre lia o livro de S. Cipriano. Às tantas, deparam com uma porta, de onde sai o diabo para levar a alma do galego. Este, coitado, vendo uma coisa tão feia à sua frente, ficou de tal modo assustado que só soube dizer:

'Jesus, mi vida, mi alma és para Dios!'

Ditas estas palavras, a porta fechou-se de repente e o diabo desapareceu. E os homens voaram para longe, o padre também. Ficaram sem vontade de lá voltar. A cova que abriram ainda hoje se pode ver.

† Origin: Vinhais, Bragança; Source: Parafita, *A Mitologia dos Mouros*, 385.

74

[9]
The Treasure of the Cerca

THE ELDERS OF GESTOSA DE Lomba used to say that, in a place called Cerca, where once the *mouros* lived, there was a buried treasure and that the *Book of St. Cyprian* said how to find it. Now, as only the priest knew how to read the book, a few men from the village asked him to go there with them so they could try to find the treasure.

The priest accepted. The worst was that one of them needed to give his soul, as exchange, to the Devil. And there were no volunteers for this. They then resolved to make this proposition to a Galician man who was working around here and he immediately accepted, for he was very poor and had a family back in his land in great need.

And they went there on a certain night. The men dug, dug, and the priest was reading the *Book of St. Cyprian*. At a certain point, they found a door, from where the Devil came out to take the soul of the Galician. This poor man, as soon as he saw such an ugly thing in front of him, was so scared that he could only say:

'Jesus, my life, my soul is for God!'

These words being said, the door was suddenly shut and the Devil disappeared. And the men went out flying to a far-away place, the priest also. They had no more interest in going back there. The ditch they opened can still be found today.

[10]
O Penedo dos Mouros †

CERTO SAPATEIRO AMBICIOSO RESOLVEU PEGAR no Livro
de São Cipriano e ir numa noite de lua cheia ao Monte das
Caldas. Pôs-se junto de um enorme penedo onde, segundo
diziam os velhos, havia um tesouro escondido que per-
tencera aos Mouros. O sapateiro abriu o livro e começou
a ler em voz alta. O penedo abriu-se em dois e o homem
entrou. Ficou tão maravilhado com as riquezas que lá havia
que nem notara o penedo a fechar-se e a prendê-lo lá dentro.

Como não voltasse a casa, a família resolveu chamar o
padre e contar-lhe o que o sapateiro tinha feito. Este, no dia
seguinte, pediu ao sacristão para o acompanhar com a cal-
deira de água benta e um raminho de alecrim até ao Monte
das Caldas. Pararam junto do penedo, o padre benzeu o
lugar, rezou três padre-nossos e três avé-marias e o penedo
abriu-se em dois. O sapateiro saiu lá de dentro meio zonzo e
o penedo voltou-se a fechar.

Levaram o homem para casa muito maltratado e, pas-
sada uma semana, ele morreu.

Constou-se pela aldeia que os Mouros lhe tinham dado
tamanha pancada que o levaram à morte. Desde então ninguém mais quis arriscar-se a tentar a sorte.

† Origin: Semelhe, Braga, Braga; Source: v.a., *Literatura Portuguesa de Tradição Oral*, LM3.

[10]
The Penedo dos Mouros (Mouros' Boulder)

A CERTAIN AMBITIOUS SHOE MAKER decided to pick up the *Book of St. Cyprian* and go, on a particular full moon night, to the Monte das Caldas. He went close to a particular boulder where, according to some old men, there was a hidden treasure belonging to the *Mouros*. The shoe maker opened the book and started to read aloud. The boulder opened in half, and the man went in. He was so marveled with the riches inside that he didn't even notice that the boulder had once again closed with him inside.

As he did not return home, his family decided to call a priest and tell him what the shoe maker had done. He, on the following day, asked the sacristan to accompany him with the bucket of holy water and a small twig of rosemary up the Monte das Caldas. They stopped near the boulder, the priest blessed the place, prayed three Our Fathers and three Hail Marys and the boulder opened in half. The shoe maker walked out from inside, very dizzy, and the boulder once again closed.

They took the man home as he was very badly treated and, after one week he died.

It was told around the village that the *Mouros* had given him such a beating that they killed him. Since then no one else has wanted to risk their luck there.

[11]
A *Fontela de Candegrelo* †

CONTA-SE EM GRIJÓ, CONCELHO DE Bragança, que um homem, que ambicionava ser muito rico, sonhou numa noite que havia um tesouro na Fontela de Candegrelo e que estava lá um figurão a guardá-lo. E no sonho também lhe foi dito que o tesouro seria seu se fosse de sua casa até à fontela sempre a ler, na ida e volta, o livro de S. Cipriano, e que bastaria dizer ao figurão onde queria que ele lhe levasse o tesouro.

O homem assim fez. Chegou lá, aparece-lhe então o figurão que lhe diz:

'Onde queres que te leve o tesouro?'

'Leva-o à minha quinta'.

O figurão pegou no tesouro e seguiu-o na direcção da quinta. E o homem lá continuava sempre a ler o livro de S. Cipriano. Acontece que, antes de chegar à quinta, o homem emocionou-se de tal modo por sentir a grande riqueza que sonhara já ali tão perto, que acabou por se enganar na leitura do livro. E ao enganar-se, diz-se que se abriu um grande buraco na terra onde entrou ele, o figurão e o tesouro. Nunca mais o voltaram a ver.

† Origin: Grijó De Parada, Bragança, Bragança; Source: Parafita, *A Mitologia dos Mouros*, 225-26.

[II]
The Fontela de Candegrelo (*Fountain of Candegrelo*)

IT IS TOLD IN GRIJÓ, county of Bragança, that a man, who wished to be very rich, one night dreamed that there was a treasure in Fontela de Candegrelo and that there was a 'figure'[5] guarding it. And the dream also told him that the treasure would be his if he was to go from his home up to the fountain, both ways, constantly reading the *Book of St. Cyprian*, and that all he had to do was tell the 'figure' where he wanted it to take the treasure.

The man thus did. He went there, and the 'figure' appeared to him and asked:

'Where do you want me to take the treasure?'

'Take it to my farm'.

The 'figure' picked the treasure up and followed him in the direction of the farm. And the man was continuously reading the *Book of St. Cyprian*. But it happened, before they got to the farm, that the man became very emotional due to feeling the great riches of which he dreamt so close, and he ended up making a mistake in the reading of the book. And when he made this mistake, it is said a great hole opened in the earth, where he, the 'figure' and the treasure all fell. He was never seen again.

---

5 Translator's note: this is a very imprecise description. 'Figurão' is just a large imposing figure; in this case it mostly just refers to a *mouro*.

[12]
Dona Mirra †

HÁ MUITO TEMPO ATRÁS, EM São Leonardo de Galafura, vivia uma moura chamada Dona Mirra que se apaixonou por um homem cristão. Não podia casar com ele, pois o seu pai possuía grande riqueza e não queria que fosse parar às mãos de um pobretanas.

Mas a moura não queria obedecer ao pai e este não teve outra escolha senão encantá-la. A lenda diz que ela ficou a guardar as riquezas do seu pai, bem como a cidade do seu povo que era feita de ouro.

Ela só poderia ser desencantada quando na gruta onde ficou presa entrasse um homem de muita coragem, que não olhasse para trás, e levasse uma broa de quatro cabeças. A gruta tem duas entradas, uma voltada para a aldeia em forma de porta e outra voltada para o rio Douro. A porta voltada para a aldeia só se abre se esse homem ler o Livro de São Cipriano do fim para o princípio. Quem lá entrasse teria de passar diversos obstáculos.

A lenda diz que houve um homem que tentou desencantar a moura. Entrou na gruta e caminhou tanto, tanto, tanto, que pegou na broa que levava e comeu uma das quatro cabeças. Um pouco mais à frente, apareceu-lhe um cavalo

† Origin: Galafura, Peso da Régua, Vila Real; Source: v.a., *Literatura Portuguesa de Tradição Oral*, ME11.

[12]
Lady Mirra

A LONG TIME AGO, IN São Leonardo de Galafura, there lived a *moura* called Lady Mirra,[6] who fell in love with a Christian man. She could not marry him, for her father had many riches, and he did not want these to fall into the hands of a pauper.

But the *moura* did not want to obey her father, and he had no other choice but to enchant her. Legend has it that she was left behind to guard the riches of her father, as well as his city and its people, which was made of gold.

She could only be disenchanted when, in the cave where she was trapped, a man of great courage entered, who would not look back, and carried with him a corn bread with four parts. The cave has two entrances, one facing the village, shaped like a door, and another facing the river Douro. The door facing the village can only be opened if a man reads the *Book of St. Cyprian* from the end to the beginning. Whoever entered would still have to face other challenges.

Legend says that there was a man who tried to disenchant the *moura*. He entered the cave and walked for such a long time that he took the corn bread and ate one of the four parts. A little further on, he came across a three-legged

6 Translator's note: although this is mostly true in the Algarve (far south of Portugal), the word `mirra' can also mean a skeleton (as well as the funerary incense myrrh).

de três pernas. O homem montou o cavalo que o levaria até à moura e mais adiante encontrou uma mulher metade cobra. Não era a moura, mas apenas um obstáculo que teria de passar para chegar até à cidade de ouro onde estava a moura que teria de beijar apaixonadamente para o encantamento acabar. Apesar da coragem que teve em chegar até ali, a verdade é que temeu e então ninguém soube mais nada do homem.

Ainda hoje a moura continua lá á espera de encontrar um homem que a tire de lá, e há quem diga que ela aparece cá fora em noites de nevoeiro para estender a sua branca roupa.

horse. The man mounted the horse for this would take him to the *moura*, and further down he met a woman who was half snake. This was not the *moura*, but rather just an obstacle he had to cross in order to reach the city of gold where the *moura* was, who he would have to passionately kiss so as to break the enchantment. Regardless of the courage he had in getting so far, the truth is that he was afraid, and as such no one ever heard from him again.

The *moura* is still there waiting to meet the man who will free her, and there are those who say that she comes out on foggy nights to put her white clothes out to dry.

[13]

Pinócros†

NO PONTO MAIS ELEVADO DA serra de S. Julião a uns 200 metros ao S dos restos de uma trincheira, facho ou atalaia que ali existem, ergue-se quasi a prumo, do lado do O, um enorme e formidavel penhasco, ao qual se dá o nome de Pinócros.

Tem varias ramificações de rocha viva, e no centro, que é o ponto mais elevado, apparece por entre as juncturas dos penêdos, e virado ao O, um buraco, de uns 15 ou 16 centímetros de diametro.

É o respiradoiro de uma immensa caverna, pois que fallando á boca do tal buraco, ouve-se a repercução do som, a grande distancia.

Ás sinuosidades da estrada, e as arestas dos rochedos que a formam, tornam impossivel a investigação d'este subterraneo, sem grandes despezas, a que ninguem se sujeita.

Não podia o nosso povo deixar de crear uma lenda a este logar, e com effeito, é tradição constante por estes sitios, que a caverna é habitada por Dona Caparixa moura encantada, que guarda alli grandes riquezas.

† Origin: Branca, Albegaria-a-Velha, Aveiro; Source: an excerpt from Pinho Leal, *Portugal Antigo e Moderno*, 7:102–3.

[13]

Pinócros

AT THE HIGHEST POINT OF the mountain of St. Julião some 200 meters south of the remains of a trench that exists there, on the west side, rising almost vertically, there is a formidable and enormous cliff, which is called Pinócros.

This has various seams of rock, and at the center, which is its highest point, it comes out of the joining of several cliffs, and turned to the west, there is a hole of some 15 or 16 centimeters in diameter.

This is the vent of an immense cavern, for if one speaks into this hole, you can hear the echo for a great distance.

The sinuosity of the entrance, and the edges of the rocks which form this, make it impossible to investigate this underground without great risk, which no one is willing to take.

Our people could not avoid creating a legend about this place, and as such, it is a tradition in these places, that the cave is inhabited by Lady Caparixa, an enchanted *moura*, who guards great treasures.

N'esta crença (ou crendice) por algumas vezes (e a última, ainda ha poucos annos) alguns mais atrevidos, teem procurado atrahir a moura cá para fóra, com evocações, esconjurios, e varias macaquices, para lhe apanharem o thesouro encantado.

E, apezar de cumprirem rigorosamente todas as formulas indicadas no Livro de S. Cypriano, e por nove noites successivas, a moira ainda não cedeu a nada d'isto, nem se dignou mostrar o seu formoso rosto, nem a mínima parte das suas riquezas, aos pretendentes.

With this belief, sometimes (and the last one was a few years ago) some more daring men have sought to attract the *moura* to come out with evocations, banishing and several foolishnesses, so as to get her enchanted treasure.

And, although they rigorously follow the formulas indicated in the *Book of St. Cyprian*, and for nine consecutive nights, the *moura* never gave in to any of this, neither showing her beautiful face, nor the smallest part of her riches to these seekers.

[14]
A Jovem Encantada †

VIVIA NO LUGAR DO QUINJO, em Castro Laboreiro, uma
princesa que tinha sido encantada sob a forma de uma serpente, e que trazia uma flor presa na boca.

Era esta princesa fabulosamente rica e estava disposta a
dividir a sua riqueza com quem a desencantasse. Como ia de
100 em 100 anos à feira de Entrime, em Espanha, altura em
que recuperava a sua forma humana, lá contou como deveria proceder a pessoa que estivesse disposta a desencantá-
la: ir ao lugar do Quinjo e dar um beijo à flor que ela, já na
forma de cobra, trazia na boca.

Se os séculos foram passando sem que aparecesse
alguém suficientemente corajoso para realizar tal façanha,
nem por isso se pode dizer que o tempo tenha apagado nos
homens a crença no tesouro escondido ou tenha esmo-
recido a fé na sua recuperação, mesmo que para tal se
tivesse de cumprir o ritual prescrito pela lenda. A cobiça
era sentimento mais forte que a repugnância e o medo, sem
contar ainda que a astúcia humana é de tal forma atrevida e
pretensiosa que só por si consegue dar, a quem dela resolva
largar mão, uma coragem inicial que na maioria dos casos,

† Origin: Castro Laboreiro, Melgaço, Viana do Castelo; Source: *Lendas do Vale do
Minho*, 77-79.

88

[14]
The Enchanted Girl

THERE LIVED IN THE PLACE of Quinjo, in Castro Laboreiro, a princess who had been enchanted under the form of a serpent, carrying a flower in her mouth.

This princess was fabulously rich and was willing to divide her riches with whomever disenchanted her. Every 100 years she would go to the market of Entrime, in Spain, at which time she would recover her human form, she said there what a person willing to disenchant her needed to do: go to the Quinjo and kiss the flower she, in the form of a snake, was carrying in her mouth.

The centuries passed, and no one brave enough appeared to perform such a feat, but time did not erase the belief in this hidden treasure or dull the faith of its gain in men, even if for this one would have to perform the ritual described in the legend. Greed was a stronger feeling than repugnance and fear, not to mention that human cunning is in such a way daring and pretentious that, by itself, can give to those willing an initial courage which in most cases, if it is not a condition for success, it is at least enough to reach the last stages of this.

se não é condição de sucesso é pelo menos de chegada à última etapa possível.

Foi assim que um dia, levados pela cobiça e apoiados na astúcia, um grupo de homens, tentaram desencantar a princesa. Se o pensaram, logo programaram a aventura, animados pelo facto de um deles conhecer os segredos do livro de S. Cipriano, que ajudaria a tomar o tesouro escondido e defendido pela serpente.

Havia contudo uma dificuldade que a todos transtornava, e que não viam meio de a superar. Como ganhar coragem para beijar a serpente? Lembraram-se então os nossos heróis de um cego que havia no lugar e que, pelo facto de não ver, não sentiria repugnância em praticar o acto. Bastante instado, mas sem saber bem ao que ia, o pobre lá anuiu em juntar-se-lhes. Reunido o grupo no local certo, no dia e hora combinados, resolveu o animador da proeza, na intenção talvez de melhor avivar os pormenores da façanha, puxar do livro e ler a lenda aos companheiros no próprio cenário onde se iria desenrolar o drama. A um dado passo da leitura, porém, fez-se ouvir um barulho medonho que, repercutindo-se pelas fragas adiante, parecia querer fendê-las para delas fazer sair a figura de um monstro.

Nem se interrogaram a respeito do estranho fenómeno: gasta a última reserva de coragem, ei-los numa corrida doida, galgando e descendo penedos, na ânsia de alcançar a segurança do lugar onde habitavam que, estranho ao facto, recuperava no sono a energia gasta num dia de luta árdua.

Sozinho no lugar do Quinjo, ficou o cego, desprotegido de tudo e de todos, e completamente amedrontado. Valeu-lhe o bordão, seu único apoio e guia, para descobrir forma

And in this way, taken by greed and supported by cunning, a group of men, tried to disenchant the princess. If they thought it, they immediately programmed their adventure, animated by the fact that one of them knew the *Book of St. Cyprian*, which would help in taking hold of the hidden treasure defended by the serpent.

There was however a difficulty that was weighing on all of them, and that there was no way around. How to gain the courage to kiss the serpent? Our heroes then remembered a blind man who lived in that place and who, given that he could not see, would not feel repugnance in practicing the act. Being urged, but not exactly knowing what he was going to, the poor man agreed to join them. They gathered at the place, at the day and hour arranged, and the organizer of the feat, perhaps intending to clear up the details, pulled out the book and the legend, retelling it to his companion in the very place where the drama was to unfold. At a certain point of the reading, however, a fearful noise was heard which, echoing through the boulders, seemed to want to crack them so as to give way to a monster.

They didn't even question the strange phenomenon; spending the last of their courage, they took off in a mad race, jumping and going down the crags, hoping to find safety in their village, which, ignorant of these events, was resting from the hardships of the day.

In the place of the Quinjo, the old man was left alone and unprotected, completely terrified. He nonetheless used his staff, his only support and guide, in order to find safe and secure ground. And, after a few days, arrived in Pereira, a small Spanish village that welcomed him.

de chegar a chão seguro e sossegado. E chegou, passados uns dias a Pereira, uma pequena povoação espanhola, que lhe deu guarida.

Depois de conhecida a aventura no lugar, nunca mais ninguém daqueles lugares pensou em repetir a proeza.

Em tempos mais recentes, um jovem, ao saber, por um pastor, da existência da serpente, logo se lembrou da sua terrível história de amor. A mãe da sua namorada contrariava muito seriamente o namoro e afeição que a filha mantinha com ele, facto que os obrigava a encontrarem-se às escondidas por entre as penedias. Não tardou muito que a mãe desse com o esconderijo dos namorados e, desesperada com a desobediência da filha, lhe lançasse esta maldição:

'Que de futuro andes de rastos como as cobras no alto do Quinjo'.

Passados dias, desapareceu a rapariga sem deixar rasto!

Associando os factos, não restaram dúvidas ao rapaz de que se tratava da namorada que cumpria o fado a que fora condenada pela mãe. A confirmá-lo, lá estava a flor que ele lhe oferecera e que ela, numa atitude garrida, trazia entre os dentes no momento em que recebera a maldição.

Desesperado pela triste sorte da jovem e também pela sua infelicidade, subiu ao monte e perguntou à serpente quais as possibilidades que havia de lhe quebrar o encanto. Respondeu-lhe esta que bastaria que ele, rapaz, tivesse a coragem de a beijar na boca. Mas, cautela, se à terceira tentativa o não conseguisse, redobraria o seu encanto e não mais podia trazê-la à vida e ao seu amor.

Voltou o rapaz mais tarde, acompanhado com gente amiga, para realizar o desencanto: porém, na altura em que

After this adventure was known in this place, no one else ever thought about repeating this feat.

In more recent times, a young man heard from a shepherd of the existence of the serpent, and immediately he was reminded of his own terrible love story. The mother of his girlfriend was seriously against the love and affection her daughter maintained for him, a fact that forced them to meet in secret and, desperate about her daughter's disobedience, cast this curse on her:

'May in the future you crawl like the snakes in the top of the Quinjo'.

After a few days, the girl disappeared without any trace!

Connecting the facts, there were no doubts for this boy that this was his girlfriend who was following the fate to which she had been condemned by her mother. And confirming it was the flower that he had given her and was in her teeth the moment she received the curse.

Desperate by the sad fate of the young woman, and also her unhappiness, he went up the mount and asked the serpent what the possibilities of breaking her enchantment were. She responded that he, the boy, needed to have courage to kiss her on the mouth. But, he should be careful, if at the third try he could not do it, he would double her enchantment and would never be able to bring back his beloved.

The boy returned later, accompanied by a few friends, to perform the disenchantment, however, when he stepped close to the serpent, it hissed and contorted in such a way that all witnessing the scene ran away. The boy did not give up, and on the second attempt was accompanied by a priest,

se aproximou da serpente, esta lançou tais silvos e contorceu-se de tal maneira que pôs em fuga todos os que presenciavam a cena. Não desistiu o namorado e, na segunda tentativa, fez-se acompanhar de um padre, para ajudar o ritual com as suas rezas, e, esquecido do que havia acontecido aos outros seus conterrâneos, de um ceguinho que, pelo facto de não ver, poderia substitui-lo no acto de beijar a serpente com menos repugnância. Repetiu-se a cena anterior e tanto o padre como o cego fugiram desaustinados.

Entendeu o rapaz que teria que ser ele sozinho, e sem a ajuda ou apoio de ninguém, mas amparado pelo amor que nutria pela jovem, a cumprir o feito. Enchendo-se de coragem, aproximou-se da serpente e, sem dificuldade de maior, deu-lhe o beijo, recebendo em troca nos seus braços a namorada. Regressaram felizes a Ribeiro de Baixo, seu lugar de nascimento, e casaram mais tarde na vila.

so as to aid in the ritual with his prayers, and, forgetting what had happened to his other companions, also a blind man who, given that he would not be repulsed, could substitute him in the act of kissing the serpent. The same scene as before was repeated and both the priest and the blind man ran away in a panic.

The boy understood that he had to do this alone, without help or aid of anyone, but solely supported by the love he felt for the young girl. Building up his courage, he approached the serpent and, without greater difficulties, kissed her, receiving in return, in his arms, his girlfriend. They returned happily to Ribeiro de Baixo, the place of their birth and later were married in that town.

Lendas do Convento da Provença†

NA MANHÃ DE S. JOÃO, aparecia ao pé da fonte uma menina com um tabuleiro de nozes, que as oferecia a quem a visse. Como ninguém aceitasse partir uma só noz, ela permanece encantada até que alguém numa manhã de S. João lhe quebre o encanto. Se acaso ninguém a visse, deixava na terra as suas pegadas.

Que também ao pé do tanque um homem viu uma serpente que procurava lamber-lhe as mãos, para assim se desencantar.

Também no velho convento, dentro de uma pedra que tinha letras que ninguém entendia, havia um encanto. Para quebrarem esse encanto, foram três homens, os quais riscaram no chão um quadrado, acenderam três velas, e começaram a ler o livro de S. Cipriano. O que aconteceu ao lerem o primeiro capítulo, não se lembrava a pessoa, mas ao lerem o segundo, o mato começou a crescer dentro da casa, e as velas apagavam-se e acendiam-se por si. No último capítulo ouviram um barulho medonho vindo do interior da pedra, bem como uma voz que dizia:

'Não tenteis tirar o encanto, senão morrereis'.

Os homens não fizeram caso, mas o barulho cresceu como se fossem montanhas a cair, e eles fugiram cheios de medo.

---

† Origin: Ribeira De Nisa, Portalegre, Portalegre; Source: Transmontano, *Subsídios para a Monografia da Ribeira de Nisa*, 37–38.

[15]
Legends of the Convent of Provença

IN THE MORNING OF ST. John, there used to appear near the fountain a little girl with a tray of nuts, which she would offer to those who saw her. As no one ever agreed to break only one nut, she remained enchanted until someone, on a St. John's morning, breaks her enchantment. If by chance no one saw her, she would leave her footsteps on the ground.

Near a water basin, a man saw a serpent that was seeking to lick his hands, so as to in this way disenchant itself.

Also, in the old convent, inside a rock which had some letters no one understood, there was an enchantment. To break this enchantment three men went there and scratched a square on the ground, lit three candles and began to read the *Book of St. Cyprian*. What happened when they read the first chapter this person did not remember, but when they read the second, the brush around them began to grow inside that house, and the candles would be blown out and re-lit by themselves. In the last chapter they heard a fearful noise coming from the interior of the rock, as well as a voice saying:

'Do not attempt to remove the enchantment, or you will die'.

The men paid no attention, but the noise grew so much that it was as if the mountains were crumbling, and they ran with fear.

[16]

O *Tear de Ouro* †

EM TEMPOS QUE LÁ VÃO, junto do regato do Martingo, onde
existe um penedo com uma grande brecha que ninguém
fora, até então, capaz de abrir, ouvia-se um barulho familiar.
Parecia o bater de um tear em pleno trabalho. Sempre que
ali passavam os transeuntes, ouviam uma labuta ininter-
rupta, o que levou o povo a acreditar que naquele local
morava uma moura encantada! Era de tal forma contínuo o
trabalho, que o povo decidiu quebrar o encanto para salvar
a pobre da moura de tão pesado fado. Se assim pensaram,
logo se reuniram junto do penedo com um entendido no
livro de S. Cipriano, para dar início ao desencantamento.

À medida que a leitura ia avançando, o penedo, lenta-
mente, ia-se abrindo, deixando descoberto aos olhares
do povo a beleza estonteante de um fantástico tesouro!
Maravilhados, fixaram os objectos que eram familiares no
seu dia-a-dia, mas que aqui refulgiam na cor do ouro tear,
lançadeiras, canelas, pentes, etc. Da moura não havia rasto!

Perante tal visão, resolveu-se deitar mão a tão grande
fortuna. O entendido no Livro de S. Cipriano havia dito que
não poderia parar a leitura, pois caso tal sucedesse, o penedo fechar-se-ia imediatamente. Assim, um outro homem,

---

† Origin: Paderne, Melgaço, Viana do Castelo; Source: Campelo, *Lendas do Vale do Minho*, 87.

[16]
The Golden Loom

IN BYGONE TIMES, NEAR THE creek of Martingo, where there is a boulder with a great crack no one until then was able to open, a familiar noise used to be heard. It seemed like the banging of a working loom. Anytime anyone passed by that place they would hear this unending labor, which led the people there to believe that in that place lived an enchanted *moura*! This work was so continuous that the villagers decided to break the enchantment to save the poor *moura* from such a heavy burden. And as soon as they thought it, they immediately got together near the boulder with an expert on the *Book of St. Cyprian*, to begin the disenchantment.

As the reading progressed, the boulder was slowly opening, revealing to the eyes of the people the astounding beauty of a fantastical treasure! Marveled, each kept an eye on objects which were familiar to their day to day activities but were here glowing with the color of gold; looms, shuttles, combs, etc., but of the *moura* not even a trace!

Before such a vision, someone decided to grab this fortune. The expert on the *Book of St. Cyprian* had said that he could not stop the reading, for if this was to happen, the boulder would close immediately. As such, another man, who had as much courage as ambition, ventured into the boulder, and was passing the gold pieces to those outside. They were doing this work, and after a great deal of wealth

que tinha tanto de coragem como de ambição, aventurou-se dentro do penedo, e entregava as peças do tesouro aos de fora. Estavam eles nestes trabalhos, e depois de muita riqueza ter saída do misterioso penedo, quando o leitor, distraído pelo esforço e impaciente na sorte, perguntou:

'Já está tudo fora?'

Nesse mesmo momento o rochedo fechou-se, prendendo no seu interior o desgraçado do homem que entrara para resgatar o tesouro!

Ouviu-se então uma voz do interior que dizia:

'Só libertarei o homem depois de restituírem ao penedo o tesouro!'

Apavorados, prometeram fazer tudo o que a voz pedira. Assim fizeram, e nunca mais tentaram conquistar o tesouro.

had come out of the mysterious boulder, the reader, distracted by the effort and impatient, asked:

'Is everything out already?'

At that very moment the boulder closed, trapping inside the poor man who had entered to take the treasure out!

A voice was then heard from the inside:

'I will only release this man after you give the treasure back to the boulder!'

Scared, they promised to do everything the voice asked. And so they did, and they never again tried to conquer the treasure.

[17]
Lenda da Anta de Paranho de Arca †

A ANTA DE PARANHO DE Arca foi erigida por uma moura e a laje que se encontra horizontalmente em cima das que servem de pilares foi lá colocada pela dita moura, trazendo-a à cabeça, a fiar numa roca e com um filho ao colo. A dita moura aparece todos os anos na madrugada de S. João a fiar uma rocada em cima da Anta e rodeada por objectos de ouro. Ao feliz mortal que lá passar em primeiro lugar será perguntado de qual gostará mais: se dos olhos da moura ou dos objectos de ouro que ela lá tem. Como todos têm dito que gostam mais dos objectos de ouro, eles têm-se transformado sempre em cinzas devido aos poderes mágicos da moura.

Só conseguirão os objectos de ouro quando se agradarem mais dos olhos da moura e não do ouro.

Consta ainda que debaixo da referida Anta existem objectos em ouro e que tal ouro se conseguirá com a reza do livro de S. Cipriano. Algumas dezenas de anos são passados, depois que 3 ou 4 sujeitos lá foram à meia noite com umas luzes rudimentares, para efectuarem no local a devida reza do livro de S. Cipriano, a fim de sacar o ouro. Conta-se que, logo ás primeiras leituras, se levantara tal ventania que todos eles fugiram atemorizados cada um para seu lado em direcção a suas casas.

† Origin: Arca, Oliveira de Frades, Viseu; Source: Cruz, *Lendas Lafonenses*, 7.

[17]
Legend of the Anta of Paranho da Arca

THE ANTA[7] DE PARANHO DE Arca was raised by a *moura*, and the slab which is horizontally on top of those that are placed as pillars was placed there by the said *moura*, who carried it on her head while she was weaving in a distaff and carrying her son. The said *moura* appears every year on St John's Eve weaving a distaff on top of the Anta surrounded by objects of gold. The happy mortal who passes by this place first will be asked which he likes the most: the eyes of the *moura* or the gold objects she has there. As all of them have said that they prefer the gold objects, these have turned to ash due to the *moura*'s magical powers.

They will only get the objects when they prefer the eyes of the *moura* and not the gold.

It is also mentioned that under the said Anta there exist several gold objects and that these can be acquired with the prayer from the *Book of St. Cyprian*. A few dozen years ago, three or four men went at midnight with some crude lights to perform in this place the proper prayer of St. Cyprian, so as to get the gold. It is told that, at the very first readings, such a wind rose up that they all ran terrified, each to his own home.

7 Translator's note: The Portuguese indigenous word for dolmen.

A *Casa dos Mouros de Cidadelha*†

CONTAM AS PESSOAS QUE NO monte de Cidadelha (concelho de Vila Pouca de Aguiar) existe o rabo de um boi e o rabo de uma vaca e por isso se diz:

'Entre o rabo de boi e o rabo de vaca está o ouro e a prata'.

Nesse monte há a casa dos mouros, tipo de uma gruta, junto ao rio Avelames, onde consta haver ouro e prata e muitos encantos. Até hoje nunca ninguém conseguiu lá entrar, mas já houve pessoas que tentaram, até com o livro de São Cipriano, mas não conseguiram.

Houve um senhor que tentou entrar e que ouviu uma voz que dizia o seguinte:

'Entrar entrarás, mas sair não sairás!'

Tiveram de tirar de lá o homem porque estava entalado na porta. E quando o tiraram estava em sangue.

† Origin: Vila Pouca de Aguiar, Vila Real; Source: Parafita, *A Mitologia dos Mouros*, 354.

[18]
The House of the Mouros of Cidadelha

PEOPLE SAY THAT IN THE mount of Cidadelha (county of Vila Pouca de Aguiar) there is the tail of an ox and the tail of a cow, and because of this it is said that:

'Between the tail of the ox and the tail of the cow, there is silver and gold'.

In those mounts there is the house of the *mouros*, a kind of cave, near the Avelames River, where it is said there is plenty of gold and silver. Until this day no one has managed to enter there, but there were people who tried, even with the *Book of St. Cyprian*, but they could not do it.

There was a man who tried to get in, and he heard a voice saying the following:

'Enter you may, but leave you may not!'

They had to pull the man out, for he became trapped in the door. And when they took him out he was all bloodied.

[19]
Lenda dos Pintainhos de Ouro †

CONTA A LENDA QUE NAS ruínas das muralhas que há perto de Cidadelha [concelho de Vila Pouca de Aguiar], em tempos antigos, no tempo dos mouros, havia lá dentro uma galinha com pintainhos de ouro. Para vê-los bastava sentar-se à porta e ler o livro de São Cipriano, que logo apareciam.

† Origin: Vila Pouca de Aguiar, Vila Pouca de Aguiar, Vila Real; Source: Parafita, *A Mitologia dos Mouros*, 354.

[19]
Legend of the Golden Chicks

LEGEND SAYS IT THAT IN the ruins of the wall near Cidadelha [county of Vila Pouca de Aguiar], in ancient times, in the
times of the *mouros*, there was a chicken with golden chicks
inside it. To see them one only had to sit by the door and read
the *Book of St. Cyprian*, and these would immediately appear.

[20]

A *Menina Encantada* †

DIZEM QUE NO SÍTIO DA Costa, termo de Mogo de Malta, do concelho de Carrazeda de Ansiães, é costume ouvir-se à meia-noite uma menina a chorar. É uma menina encantada. E para se lhe tirar o encanto é preciso ir lá, à meia-noite, e ler o livro de S. Cipriano. E quem o ler não se pode enganar, nem ter medo. Caso contrário, a pessoa que se aventure ficará tolhida.

Ainda não houve até à data quem tivesse coragem para lá ir. Mas bem gostariam, porque a pessoa que fizesse como manda a lenda ficaria muito rica.

† Origin: Mogo De Malta, Carrazeda de Ansiães, Bragança; Source: Parafita, *A Mitologia dos Mouros*, 232.

[20]

The Enchanted Girl

IT IS SAID THAT IN the place of the Costa, around Mogo de Malta, county of Carrazeda de Ansiães, it is normal to hear, around midnight, a girl crying. This is an enchanted girl. In order to break her enchantment, it is necessary to go there, at midnight, and read the *Book of St. Cyprian*. And whoever reads it cannot make a mistake, nor have fear. Otherwise this person will be paralyzed.

To this day there was no one with the courage to go there. But many would like to, for the person who did this, according to the legend, would become very rich.

[21]

A *Menina Tecedeira* †

NO LUGAR DA FONTE DO Lameiro de Cima, onde agora há muitas casas, mas dantes não havia, e só lá estava a fonte, dizia-se que aparecia uma menina, e que era tecedeira, pois sentia-se bater o tear. E o tear era de oiro. Até chegaram também a ver lá lume de ela estar lá.

Mas diz que, para a verem, haviam de ir lá na noite de S. João e dar-lhe umas certas falas com palavras que estavam no livro de S. Cipriano. Só que ninguém conseguia dizê-las. Os meus irmãos chegaram a ir lá para a verem no S. João, mas também não a viram.

† Origin: Vilas Boas, Vila Flor, Bragança; Source: Parafita, *Património Imaterial do Douro*, 2:284.

[21]
The Weaving Girl

IN THE PLACE OF LAMEIRA de Cima, where now there are a great deal of houses, but back in the day there were none and the only thing there was a fountain, it used to be said that a girl would appear there, and that she was a weaver, for one could hear the beating of a loom. And this was a golden loom. A light was even seen there when the girl was in.

But it is said that, in order to see her, one should go on St. John's Eve and say certain words which were in the *Book of St. Cyprian*. But no one ever managed to say them. My brothers went there to see her on St. John's Eve, but they didn't see her.

[22]
A *Lenda do Cabeço da Moura* †

CONTA A LENDA QUE EM Penouços, Paradela do Vouga, existe uma Moura encantada dentro de duas pedras, pelo que esse lugar se chama Cabeço da Moura. Dizem os mais velhos que dentro dessas pedras existem também objectos em ouro cobiçados pelas pessoas da terra. Já houveram tentativas por parte de várias pessoas consideradas corajosas mas até agora nada conseguiram desvendar. Diz-se também que para tal feito são precisas 5 pessoas que se devem colocar nas pontas do 'Cinco sem mão' ‡ e um deles lê o livro de S. Cipriano.

† Origin: Paradela, Sever do Vouga, Aveiro; Source: Silva, *Sever do Vouga*, 10–11.
‡ A Portuguese phonetic play on *sino saimão*/sign of Solomon.

[22]

The Legend of the Cabeço da Moura (Moura's Mound)

LEGEND SAYS THAT IN PENOUÇOS, Paradela do Vouga, there
is an enchanted *Moura* inside two rocks, and due to that, that
place is called Cabeço da Moura. The elders say that inside
those rocks there are also objects coveted by the people of
that land. There were some attempts by people considered
brave, but up to this point they couldn't discover anything. It
is said that to do this one needs five people who should place
themselves at the tip of the 'five without a hand' (*sino saimão*)
and one of them reads from the *Book of St. Cyprian*.

[23]
Lenda da Cabreia †

HÁ UMA LENDA QUE DIZ terem os mouros deixado cair uma grade de ouro no poço mais fundo da Cabreia, em Silva Escura. Segundo a lenda, é possivel recuperá-la com dois bois pretos e o livro de S. Cipriano, com uma reza que tem no dito livro.

Foram os mouros que deram início à lenda, quando habitaram no ponto mais alto ao lado da Cabreia, no Castro.

Dizem ainda que há muitos anos um homem tentou tirar a grade com uma junta de bois, conforme os bois iam puxando, o homem ia praguejando e quando a grade já cá estava fora, o homem disse: 'Graças a Deus, já cá estás fora', e a grade arrastou com ela os bois para o fundo do poço.

† Origin: Silva Escura, Sever do Vouga, Aveiro; Source: Silva, *Sever do Vouga*, 9.

[23]
Legend of the Cabreira

THERE IS A LEGEND THAT says that the *mouros* dropped a golden harrow in one of the deepest wells of the Cabreira, in Silva Escura. According to the legend, it is possible to recover it with two black oxen and the *Book of St. Cyprian*, with a prayer that is in this book.

The *mouros* started this legend, when they lived in the highest point next to the Cabreira, in the Castro.

It is further said that many years ago a man tried to take the harrow out with a pair of oxen, and as the oxen were pulling, the man would be swearing and when the harrow was out, the man said: 'Thank God, you're out', and the harrow dragged the oxen to the bottom of well.

[24]
O *Tesouro, a Moura e o Diabo* †

NOS EIVADOS, CONCELHO DE MIRANDELA, arrancaram uma oliveira por sonharem com um tesouro debaixo dela. Depois de muito ler no Livro de São Cipriano e de muito cavar, apareceu a moura e também o Diabo, que ninguém aguentou pé firme, e por isso todos arrebatados por grande vendaval foram projectados a grandes distâncias, ficando o tesouro encantado como estava.

† Origin: Mirandela, Bragança; Source: Parafita, *A Mitologia dos Mouros*, 273.

[24]
The Treasure, the Moura and the Devil

IN EIVADOS, COUNTY OF MIRANDELA, they tore out an olive tree for thinking that there was a treasure under it. After reading a lot from the *Book of St. Cyprian* and digging a great deal, a *moura* appeared, as well as the Devil, and no one could stand their ground, and because of this, taken by a great wind, they were projected to a great distance, and the treasure was left enchanted.

[25]
O *Penedo dos Namorados* †

NUM LUGAR CHAMADO FELGUEIRAS, PERTENCENTE à freguesia de Mancelos, existe um penedo conhecido como Penedo dos Namorados. Dizem que debaixo daquele penedo há muito ouro escondido. Só o consegue abrir quem ler o Livro de São Cipriano.

Um dia, um homem, no intuito de ficar com o ouro, começou a ler o livro e, quando chegou a meio, foi impedido de continuar devido a uma tempestade muito forte. O homem, assustado, desistiu de o ler.

A partir desse dia, nunca mais ninguém tentou abrir esse penedo.

† Origin: Travanca, Amarante, Porto; Source: v.a., *Literatura Portuguesa de Tradição Oral*, TE12.

[25]
The Penedo dos Namorados (Lovers' Boulder)

IN A PLACE CALLED FELGUEIRAS, belonging to the parish of Mancelos, there is a boulder known as Penedo dos Namorados. It is said that under that boulder there is a lot of hidden gold. One can only open it if one reads from the *Book of St. Cyprian.*

One day a man, intending to take the gold, started to read the book and, when he got to the middle, was stopped by a strong storm. The man, frightened, gave up on reading.

From that day on, no one else ever attempted to open that boulder.

[26]
Lenda da Fonte do Ouro †

NA BEIRA GRANDE, HÁ A Fonte do Ouro, que tem esse
nome porque, ao que contavam os antigos, um certo sujeito
sonhou que ali havia moedas de ouro, mas que teria de ir lá
encontrá-las a ler o Livro de S. Cipriano.

Ele então foi lá, e as moedas aparecer apareceram, mas
nessa altura diz que, com atrapalhação, se enganou no que
estava a ler, e que, por isso, se sentiu tão mal, que teve de
fugir sem levar as moedas. E ninguém mais as viu.

† Origin: Beira Grande, Carrazeda de Ansiães, Bragança; Source: Parafita, *Património Imaterial do Douro*, 2:164.

[26]
Legend of the Fonte do Ouro (Fountain of Gold)

IN BEIRA GRANDE THERE IS the Fonte do Ouro, and this has this name because, according to the elders, a certain individual dreamt that there were gold coins in that place, but that to find them he would have to read the *Book of St. Cyprian.*

And so he went there, and the coins did appear, but at that time it is said that, with such distraction, he made a mistake in what he was reading, and because of this, he felt so indisposed that he had to flee without the coins. And no one ever saw them again.

[27]
O Ouro do Monte de Santa Marinha†

NO MONTE DE SANTA MARINHA, da freguesia da Barroca
Funda, Lixa, existe um penedo onde dizem haver ouro
escondido.

Para se conseguir abrir esse penedo e retirar o ouro,
a pessoa que o quiser tentar, tem que ler o Livro de São
Cipriano de trás para a frente. Dizem que, ao ler o livro,
aparecem muitos animais, dos mais esquisitos que existem
e existiram, que assustam quem o está a ler. O livro deve ser
lido à meia-noite e com a luz da lua. A pessoa que o estiver
a ler não pode ter medo dos animais, pois, caso tenha, não
conseguirá abrir o penedo nem ter o ouro.

Até hoje ainda não foi aberto, pois as pessoas têm medo
daquilo que possa acontecer.

† Origin: Travanca, Amarante, Porto; Source: v.a., *Literatura Portuguesa de Tradição Oral*, TE11.

[27]
The Gold of the Monte de Santa Marinha (Saint Marinha's Mount)

IN THE MONTE DE SANTA Marinha, in the parish of Barroca Funda, Lixa, there is a boulder that is said to contain hidden gold.

In order to open this boulder and take the gold, the person wanting to do this must read the *Book of St. Cyprian* from the back to the front. It is said that who reads the book will see many strange animals, which exist or existed, that will frighten the person reading. The book should be read at midnight and in the moonlight. The person reading cannot be afraid of these animals, for, if she is, she will neither be able to open the boulder nor have the gold.

Until today it has not been opened because people are afraid of what might happen.

[28]
O Tesouro de Lamelas †

NO LUGAR DE LAMELAS, DO concelho de Ribeira de Pena, há um sítio a que o povo chama 'Alto das Lameiras' e que tem ao pé o 'Outeiro dos Mouros' e mais abaixo a 'Praça dos Mouros'. Diziam os antigos que na noite de S. João, pela meia-noite, quem lá fosse a ler, com atenção e com devoção, mas sem medo, o livro de S. Cipriano, havia de descobrir o sítio onde está um tesouro composto por uma grade, uma charrua e um cambão, tudo em ouro.

Numa ocasião, isto há mais de cinquenta anos, foram lá uns rapazes mais corajosos de Ribeira de Pena, levados pela ideia e pela ambição do tesouro. Entre eles ia o Sr. José Joaquim Gaspar Andrade Borges, que nasceu em 1918. E descobriram então várias inscrições numa fraga. Alguns acreditam que elas têm a ver com o tesouro. Quer tenham, quer não tenham, o certo é que esta descoberta fez nascer o que é hoje conhecido como o Santuário Rupestre de Lamelas.

† Origin: Ribeira de Pena, Vila Real; Source: Parafita, *A Mitologia dos Mouros*, 315.

[28]
The Treasure of Lamelas

IN THE PLACE OF LAMELAS, in the county of Ribeira Grande, there is a place which the locals call 'Alto das Lameiras', and close to this there is the 'Outeiro dos Mouros' (Mouros' hill) and further down the 'Praça dos Mouros' (Mouros' plaza). The elders say that on St. John's Eve, around midnight, whoever went there to read, with great care but no fear, the *Book of St. Cyprian*, would discover the place where there is a treasure made up of a harrow, a cart, and a yoke, all made of gold.

On one occasion, over fifty years ago, some brave boys from Ribeira da Pena went there, driven by the ambition of this treasure. Among them was Mr. José Joaquim Gaspar Andrade Borges, who was born in 1918. And they found several inscriptions on a boulder. Some believe these have to do with the treasure. Whether they do or not, this discovery was at the origin of the Rock Sanctuary of Lamelas.

Lenda do Bezerro de Ouro (versão A) †

É CORRENTE NO POVO, NÃO só na aldeia de Cimo de Vila (da Castanheira, concelho de Chaves), mas também de outras aldeias à roda do Castelo do Mau Vizinho, a crença de lá existir um encanto, que é, nada mais nada menos, um bezerro de ouro maciço.

Conta-se que um ambicioso português, ansioso por deitar as unhas ao bezerro de ouro, contratou um galego para ir com ele quebrar o encanto, com a condição expressa de não se falar em Deus. Com o livro de S. Cipriano fizeram as rezas obrigatórias. A dada altura surgiu o bezerro, tão alentado que o galego não conteve o seu espanto admirativo e disse:

'Jesus...!'

Foi o bastante para que o bezerro rebentasse em carvões.

† Origin: Cimo De Vila Da Castanheira, Chaves, Vila Real; Source: Parafita, *A Mitologia dos Mouros*, 234–235.

[29]
Legend of the Golden Calf (Version A)

IT IS COMMON AMONG THE locals, not only in the villages of Cimo de Vila (from Castanheira, county of Chaves), but also around the other villages near Castelo do Mau Vizinho, the belief that an enchantment exists there, which is nothing other than a calf made of solid gold.

It is told that an ambitious Portuguese man, eager to place his hands on the golden calf, hired a Galician man to go with him to break the enchantment, with the express condition that no one was to talk of God. Having the *Book of St. Cyprian*, they made the mandatory prayers. At a given point the calf appeared, this in such a way that the Galician could not contain his admiration and said:

'Jesus...!'

This was enough to make the calf explode into coal.

[30]
Lenda do Bezerro de Ouro (versão B)†

UM PORTUGUÊS COBIÇOSO DO TESOURO encantado em forma de bezerro de ouro combinou com um padre, armado de estola, e munidos de uma panela com unguento humano, irem quebrar o encanto.

Lá foram com o indispensável e famoso livro de S. Cipriano. Feita a leitura do texto apropriado ao caso, surgiu o bezerro guiado pelo inimigo. A atarantação foi tão grande, tanto do padre leitor como do adjunto português cobiçoso, que se entornou a panela e o unguento foi escaldar o padre em vez de escaldar o inimigo.

A um 'valha-me Deus' o bezerro e o diabo que o guiava desapareceram num ápice.

---

† Origin: Cimo De Vila Da Castanheira, Chaves, Vila Real; Source: Parafita, *A Mitologia dos Mouros*, 235.

[30]
Legend of the Golden Calf (Version B)

A PORTUGUESE MAN EAGER TO find an enchanted treasure in the form of a golden calf, arranged with a priest, armed with a stole and with a pan of human fat, to go break its enchantment.

They went there with the indispensable and famous *Book of St. Cyprian*. Having read the appropriate text for the occasion, the calf appeared, being guided by the enemy.[8] And the fright was so great, both from the priest and the greedy Portuguese, that the pan of fat was spilled and burnt the priest, instead of the enemy.

By saying a 'God help me', the calf and the Devil guiding it disappeared in an instant.

8 Translator's note: the Devil.

[31]
O Bezerro de Ouro †

NUMA OCASIÃO, UM HOMEM MUITO ambicioso convenceu um padre das redondezas a irem os dois ao Castelo do Mau Vizinho quebrar o encanto do bezerro de ouro – aquele que dizem encontrar-se nas ruínas do castelo e, desse modo, resgatar o tesouro. A ideia era, em conjunto, porem em prática os rituais de desencantamento então em voga.

Para tal, muniram-se de uma panela com unguento humano e do famoso Livro de São Cipriano. O padre pôs a sua estola ao pescoço... e lá foram.

Chegados ao castelo, e enquanto o homem ambicioso segurava na panela do unguento, o padre iniciou as leituras. Mal acabou de ler, eis que lhes surge à frente um grande bezerro guiado pelo Demónio!

Diz a lenda que, perante tal visão, ficaram ambos tão apavorados que o unguento, em vez de escaldar o Demónio, foi escaldar o padre. E que ele, ao ver-se em tamanha aflição, ergueu as mãos e gritou:

'Valha-me Deus!'

Com este 'Valha-me Deus', tudo voltou ao lugar. O silêncio caiu de novo sobre as ruínas do castelo. O bezerro e o Demónio desapareceram. Até hoje.

† Origin: Cimo De Vila Da Castanheira, Chaves, Vila Real; Source: Parafita, *O Tesouro dos Maruxinhos*, 18.

[31]
The Golden Calf

ON ONE OCCASION, A VERY ambitious man convinced a priest from where he lived to go with him to the Castelo do Mau Vizinho to break the enchantment of the golden calf – the one they say is near the ruins of the castle, and, in that way, recover the treasure. The idea was to, together, put into practice the disenchantment rituals so much in fashion.

To do this, they armed themselves with a pan of human fat and the famous *Book of St. Cyprian*. The priest placed the stole around his neck... and there they went.

Arriving at the castle, and while the ambitious man held the pan of fat, the priest began his readings. As soon as he finished, the great calf appeared before him, guided by the Devil!

The legend says that, before such a vision, they were both so frightened that the fat, instead of burning the Devil, burned the priest. And he, seeing himself in such a bind, raised his hands and shouted:

'God help me!'

With this 'God help me', everything returned to its place. Silence once again fell over the ruins of the castle. The calf and the Devil disappeared. Until this day.

BIBLIOGRAPHY

Campelo, Álvaro. *Lendas do Vale do Minho*. Valença: Associa-
ção de Municípios do Vale do Minho, 2002.

Consiglieri Pedroso, Zófimo. *Contribuições para uma Mitologia Popular Portuguesa e Outros Escritos Etnográficos.*
Lisbon: Publicações Dom Quixote, 2007.

Contreiras, Maria da Rocha. *As Lendas de Mouras Encantadas.*
Master's thesis. Universidade do Algarve, 2004.

Cruz, Julio. *Lendas Lafonenses*. Vouzela: AVIZ/Clube de Am-
biente e Património da Escola Secundária de Vouzela/
ADRL, 1998.

Ferreira, Joaquim Alves. *Lendas e Contos Infantis*. Vila Real:
Author's edition, 1999.

Feyjoó y Montenegro, Benito Geronymo. 'De la vana y per-
niciosa aplicación a buscar tesoros escondidos'. In *Cartas
Eruditas, y Curiosas, En Que Por la Mayor Parte, Se Continua el Desígnio del Theatro Critico Universal Inpugnando,
ò Reduciendo à Dudosa, Varias Opiniones Comunes.* 5 vols.
Madrid: Imprenta Real de la Gaceta, 1777.

Fonseca Henriquez, Francisco da. *Medicina Lusitana, e Soc-
corro Delphico aos clamores da Natureza humana, para total
profligação de seus males*. Amsterdam: Casa de Miguel
Diaz, 1710.

Frank, Roslyn M. 'Evidence in Favor of the Palaeolithic
    Continuity Refugium Theory (PCRT): Hamalau and its
    Linguistic and Cultural Relatives'. Part I, *Insula* 4 (2008):
    91–131.
————. 'Evidence in Favor of the Palaeolithic Continuity
    Refugium Theory (PCRT): Hamalau and its Linguistic and
    Cultural Relatives'. Part 2, *Insula* 5 (2009): 89–133.
————. 'Recovering European Ritual Bear Hunts: A Com-
    parative Study of Basque and Sardinian Ursine Carnival
    Performances'. *Insula* 3 (2008): 41–97.
Frazão, Fernanda and Morais, Gabriela. *Portugal, Mundo dos
    Mortos e das Mouras Encantadas.* 3 vols. Lisbon: Apenas
    Livros, 2009–2010.
Leitão, José. *The Book of St. Cyprian: The Sorcerer's Treasure.*
    N.p.: Hadean Press, 2014.
————. 'Searching for Cyprian in Portuguese Ethnogra-
    phy'. In *Cypriana: Old World*, edited by Alexander Cum-
    mins, Jesse Hathaway Diaz, and Jennifer Zahrt, 117–62.
    2016. Reprint Seattle: Revelore Press, 2017.
López, Jesús Suárez. *Tesoros, Ayalgas y Chalgueiros: La Fiebre
    Del Oro en Asturias.* Grijó: Muséu del Pueblu d'Asturies,
    2001.
Marques, Amália. *Mouras, Mouros e Mourinhos Encantados em
    Lendas do Norte e Sul de Portugal.* Master's thesis, Univer-
    isdade Aberta, 2013.
Missler, Peter. 'Las Hondas Raíces del Ciprianillo. Tercera
    parte: las "Gacetas"'. *Culturas Populares: Revista Electrónica*
    4 (2007): 17.
Missler, Peter. 'Tradición y parodia en el Millonario de San
    Ciprián, primer recetario impreso para buscar tesoros

en Galicia: Las hondas raíces del Ciprianillo: 1ª Parte'. *Culturas Populares: Revista Electrónica* 2 (2006): 8.

Morgado, Isabel. *Viagens ao Imaginário*. Torres Vedras: Centro de Formação das Escolas de Torres Vedras, 1999.

Nova, Maria Manuela Neves Casinha. *As Lendas do Sobrenatural da Região do Algarve*. 2 vols. Lisbon: Universidade de Lisboa, 2012.

Otto, Bernd-Christian and Stausberg, Michael, eds. *Defining Magic: A Reader*. Sheffield: Equinox Publishing, 2012.

Paiva, José Pedro. *Bruxaria e Superstição num País Sem 'Caça às Bruxas': Portugal 1600–1774*. Lisbon: Editorial Notícias 2002.

Parafita, Alexandre. *A Mitologia dos Mouros: Lendas, Mitos, Serpentes, Tesouros*. Vila Nova de Gaia: Gailivro, 2006.

————. *O Tesouro dos Maruxinhos: Mitos e Lendas para os Mais Novos*. Lisboa: Oficina do Livro, 2008.

————. *Património Imaterial do Douro*. 3 vols. Peso da Régua: Fundação Museu do Douro, 2010–2014.

Parafita Correia, Alexandre José. *Mouros Míticos em Trás-os-Montes: Contributos para um estudo dos mouros no imaginário rural a partir de textos da literatura popular de tradição oral*. PhD thesis, Universidade de Trás-os-Montes e Alto Douro, n.d.

Pedrosa, José Manuel. 'El Cuento de El Tesoro Soñado (AT1645) y el Complejo Leyendístico de El Becerro de Oro'. *E. L. O.* 4 (1998): 127–57.

————, Palacios, César Javier, and Marcos, Elías Rubio. *Héroes, Santos, Moros y Brujas: Leyendasépicas, históricas e mágicas de la tradició de Burgos*. Burgos: Gráficas Aldecoa, 2001.

Pinho Leal, Augusto Soares d'Azevedo Barbosa de. *Portugal Antigo e Moderno*. 12 vols. Lisboa: Livraria Editora Tavares Cardoso & Irmão, 1873–1890.

Silva, José Luciano de Figueiredo. *Sever do Vouga*. N.p.: Câmara Municipal de Sever do Vouga, n.d.

Tengarrinha, Margarida. *Da Memória do Povo*. Lisboa: Colibri, 1999.

Transmontano, Maria Tavares. *Subsídios para a Monografia da Ribeira de Nisa*. Portalegre: Author's edition, 1989.

Vasconcelos, José Leite de. *Etnografia Portuguesa*. 10 vols. Lisboa Imprensa Nacional – Casa da Moeda, 2006–2007.

————. *Tradições Populares de Portugal*. Porto: Livraria Portuense de Clavel & C.a – Editores 1882.

Vaz da Silva, Francisco. 'Extraordinary Children, Werewolves, and Witches in Portuguese Folk Tradition'. In *Witchcraft, Mythologies and Persecutions: Demons, Spirits, Witches*, edited by Gabor Klaniczay and Éva Pócs, 255–68. Budapest: Central European University Press, 2008.

————. 'Iberian Seventh-Born Children, Werewolves, and the Dragon Slayer: A Case Study in the Comparative Interpretation of Symbolic Praxis and Fairytales'. *Folklore* 114.3 (2003): 335–53.

V.a. *Literatura Portuguesa de Tradição Oral*. N.p.: Projecto Vercial – Universidade de Trás-os-Montes e Alto Douro, 2003.

Vicente, Gil. *Exortação da Guerra*. Lisbon: Faculdade de Letras de Universidade de Lisboa – Centro de Estudos de Teatro, n.d.

José Leitão is a Portuguese Saint Cyprian devotee. He holds a PhD in experimental physics from the University of Delft and has finished a second Master's degree in religious studies at the University of Amsterdam in 2016. His current research interests focus on using ethnographic and folkloric methodologies to map the concepts of folk magic, sorcery, and witchcraft as described in the records of the Portuguese Inquisition. He produced the first English translation of one of the traditional Portuguese grimoires attributed to Saint Cyprian, *The Book of St. Cyprian: The Sorcerer's Treasure* (Hadean Press, 2014), and is currently working on collecting manuscripts and low circulation Portuguese Saint Cyprian literature to further progress the international understanding of the Sorcerer Saint.

ABOUT THE SERIES

The Folk Necromancy in Transmission series examines the folk magical expressions and interrelations of the histories, philosophies, and practices of spirit conjuration, ghost-lore, eschatology, charm-craft, demonology, and the mass of rituals, protocols, and beliefs signalled by the terms 'nigromancy', 'necromancy' and their various equivalents in traditions across the world.

Here we take the canonical and reveal the folkloric expression; here the historical text inspires new practice and discourse. This series will not simply chart the print history of grimoires, or their socio-political context, but explore their actual magical usage. Within this exploration comes discourse on and with those traditions, extant or extinct, deemed 'necromantic' that are passed through oral transmission.

With these goals in mind, we are proud to be working currently towards future publications on the Biblical Magi as mythic magician-ancestors, an anthology on women's necromancy and female exorcists, further work on the Good SAINT CYPRIAN of Antioch, and yet the work is only beginning...

Raising the dead, we acknowledge the raising of necromancy itself, for it is still the breath of the reader that gives new life to the Dead from the bones of old Books. This is a folk necromancy that is at once extant and revived, inspired and yet-to-be. Here we walk hand-in-hand with the patrons of this particular Art.

ABOUT THIS VOLUME

In this second release of *Folk Necromancy in Transmission*, scholar and Cyprian devotee José Leitão has translated folk stories and legends surrounding the Saint and his infamous book, directly from Iberian sources. This transmission of cultural, historical, and geographic context is not only translated into English by Leitão, but presented alongside the original Portuguese. Revelore's commitment to side-by-side translation preserves and honors the vital mercuric relationship between the terroir of the original tongue and the newly wrought text. Such efforts of translation remind us no interpretation is ever singular or monolithic. As such, both in form and function, the 'Immaterial Book' presents a landscape of contextualized culture pertaining to the Saint often lost in modern narrow portraits or scant mentions. Here a recognition for the historicity and transmission of the Saint is demanded of the reader as something outside familiarity or private revelations – indeed it bathes the Saint in the ink-blood of Book, and Work, that is never finished...

The Immaterial Book of St. Cyprian was typeset in Andada HT Pro (Carolina Giovagnoli), Borges (Alejandro Lo Celso), Alize (Tom Grace), Trinité Titling (Bram de Does), Miniscule (Thomas Huot-Marchand), & Solitaire MVB Pro (Mark van Bronkhorst).

Lightning Source UK Ltd.
Milton Keynes UK
UKHW010352201020
371846UK00003B/822